Model of United States Revenue Brig "Washington"

Photograph by M. Rosenfeld. Larchmont Yacht Club Collection

THE BUILT-UP
SHIP MODEL

Charles G. Davis

DOVER PUBLICATIONS, INC.
NEW YORK

Published in Canada by General Publishing Company, Ltd.,
30 Lesmill Road, Don Mills, Toronto, Ontario.
Published in the United Kingdom by Constable and Company, Ltd.

This Dover edition, first published in 1989,
is an unabridged republication of the work originally published as
Publication Number Twenty-five of the
Marine Research Society, Salem, Massachusetts, in 1933.

Manufactured in the United States of America
Dover Publications, Inc.,
31 East 2nd Street,
Mineola, N.Y. 11501

Library of Congress Cataloging-in-Publication Data

Davis, Charles G. (Charles Gerard), 1870–1959.
The built-up ship model / Charles G. Davis. — Dover ed.
p.   cm.
Reprint. Originally published: Salem, Mass. :
Marine Research Society, 1933.
(Publication number twenty-five of the Marine Research Society)
ISBN 0-486-26174-3
1. Ship models.   2. Lexington (Brig)   I. Title.   II. Series:
Publication . . . of the Marine Research Society ; no. 25.
VM298.D25   1989
623.8'201—dc20   89-37267
CIP

PREFACE

MANY requests having been received from modelers of little ships fired with an ambition to build a regular built-up model, to be constructed in the same way that real ships were built, the author has essayed this work. He has not been deluded into thinking that it is going to be an easy job, either in the telling or the doing, and all amateurs are warned, here and now, not to tackle this job before attempting some simpler type of craft than a large ship, for there is nothing more complicated under the sun than the building of a large vessel. It is an inspiring sight, when completed, to one who understands the complications encountered, but there will be many headaches during the building.

Be wary of departing from the methods described in order to adopt alluring quick methods and time-saving cut-offs. It is wise to remember that the shipbuilding industry is many centuries old and many have tried what seemed like quicker methods. Hundreds of shipbuilders, however, have finally boiled down their methods to the manner of construction here described as being the simplest and best way to build a ship. I have always had better luck in building my miniature ships just as the real ships were put together, and if "the proof of the pudding is in the eating," I have, I think, proved this point; for I built a ship model as I wrote this story so that when expediencies had to be resorted to, owing to the small size of the ship and my bulk preventing me from getting inside the hull, as a man would have done in the building of a real ship, I could the better describe the modus operandi and not overlook any vital point in the work.

Photographs were taken from time to time which are herewith reproduced. These will also help to prove the efficiency of this mode of construction.

In selecting a vessel after which to build a model, I picked out the United States brig *Lexington*, mounting sixteen 4-pounders, which was so renamed to commemorate the shedding of American blood in the battle at Lexington, on April 19, 1775.

The *Lexington* was one of the small fleet of fourteen merchant vessels that were hastily converted into war vessels, at Philadelphia, in 1775. Most of these vessels, under command of Commodore Esek Hopkins, sailed as a squadron to the West Indies and attacked the British base of supplies on the island of New Providence.

The *Lexington* sailed later under Capt. John Barry, on April 7, 1776, and while cruising off the capes of Virginia fell in with the armed sloop *Edward*, a tender to the British man-of-war *Liverpool*, and after a sharp fight, in which the sloop was badly cut up and many of her crew killed, the *Edward* surrendered. Later in that year the *Lexington*, under Capt. James Hallock, sailed to the West Indies, and while returning, in October, was captured by the British thirty-two gun frigate *Pearl*. The weather, at the time of the capture, was so stormy that only five of the crew of the *Lexington* were taken out of her and transfered to the frigate in the boat that brought the prize crew on board the brig. On the following night the brig's men overpowered the prize crew and brought the *Lexington* safely into Baltimore.

In the spring of 1777 the *Lexington* sailed across the Atlantic to France, where she arrived in April. With the brig *Reprisal*, Capt. L. Wicks, that had taken Dr. Benjamin Franklin to France, the year before, and a ten-gun cutter named the *Dolphin*, under Lieut. S. Nicholson, the *Lexington* made a cruise from June to August in the Bay of Biscay, the English Channel, and around Ireland, capturing fourteen vessels in five days, and recapturing the ship *Crawford* with 110 prisoners, who thus regained their freedom.

Returning from France, in charge of Capt. H. Johnston, the *Lexington* was captured on September 20, 1777, by the British cutter *Alert*, after an engagement of three and one-half hours during which all the ammunition on board the *Lexington* was used and she was surrendered to save the lives of her crew. The armament of the *Alert* was ten guns and two swivels and she carried a crew of sixty men. The British account of the action relates that after two hours fighting the *Lexington* crippled the *Alert's* rigging and then made off, but the *Alert* smartly repaired and renewing the chase soon came up with the *Lexington* which, through lack of ammunition passively endured the *Alert's* broadside for an hour and a half, and then struck her colors, with seven killed and eleven wounded. The *Alert* lost two killed and three wounded. She was a 10-gun cutter, launched at Dover in 1777, of 183 tons.

The dimensions of the *Lexington* were: length on gun deck, 90 feet 0 inches; length on keel, 76 feet 5 inches; beam, 22 feet 8 inches; depth, 9 feet 0 inches; tonnage, 166 tons.

DISMANTLED BRITISH 10-GUN BRIG-OF-WAR

PLATES

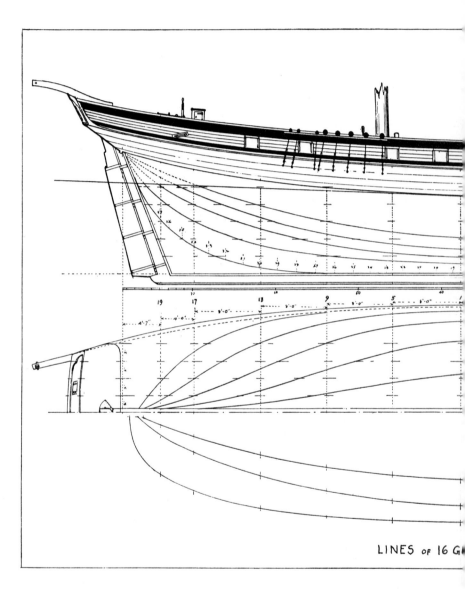

LINES of 16 G

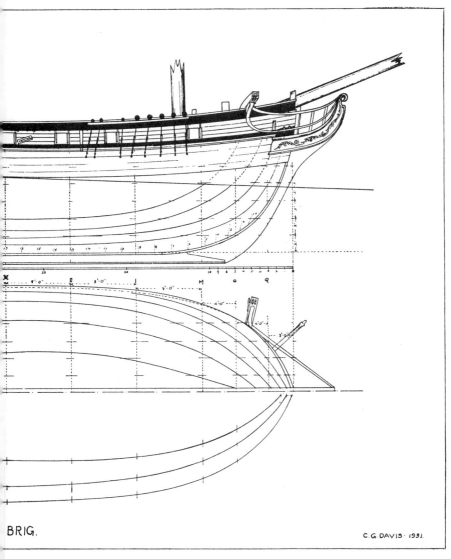

BRIG.

PLATE I

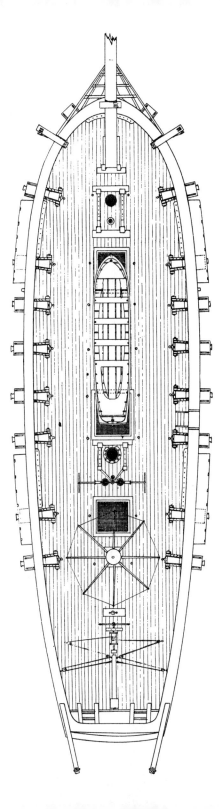

Plate II

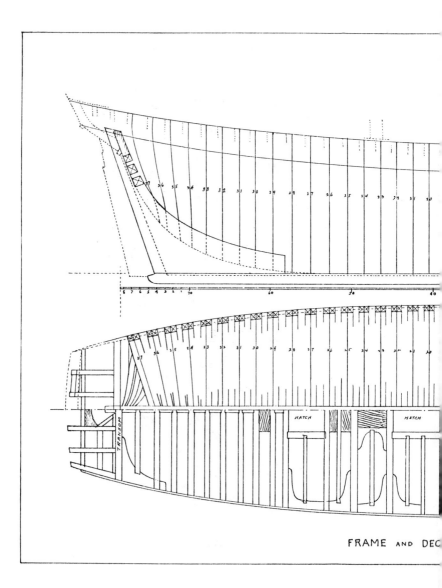

FRAME AND DEC

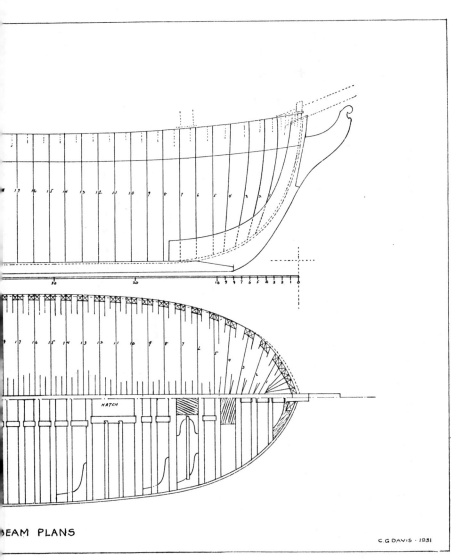

BEAM PLANS

PLATE III

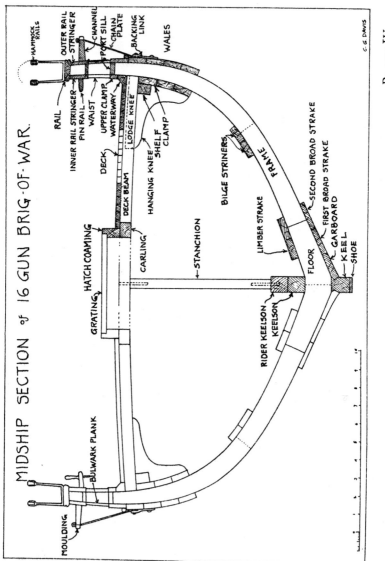

MIDSHIP SECTION of 16 GUN BRIG-OF-WAR.

HAMMOCK RAILS
OUTER RAIL
STRINGER
CHANNEL
PORT SILL
CHAIN PLATE
BACKING LINK
WALES
RAIL
INNER RAIL STRINGER
PIN RAIL
WAIST
DECK
UPPER CLAMP
WATERWAY
LODGE KNEE
HANGING KNEE
SHELF
CLAMP
DECK BEAM
BILGE STRINGERS
FRAME
SECOND BROAD STRAKE
FIRST BROAD STRAKE
GARBOARD
KEEL
SHOE
LIMBER STRAKE
STANCHION
CARLING
FLOOR
KEELSON
RIDER KEELSON
HATCH COAMING
GRATING
BULWARK PLANK
MOULDING

C. G. DAVIS

PLATE IV

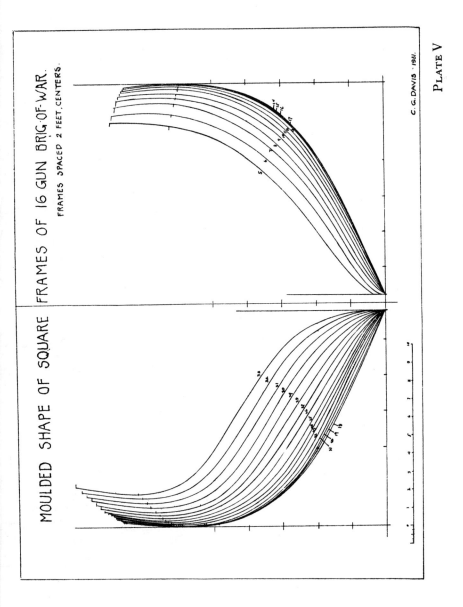

MOULDED SHAPE OF SQUARE FRAMES OF 16 GUN BRIG·OF·WAR.

FRAMES SPACED 2 FEET. CENTERS.

C. G. DAVIS · 1911.

PLATE V

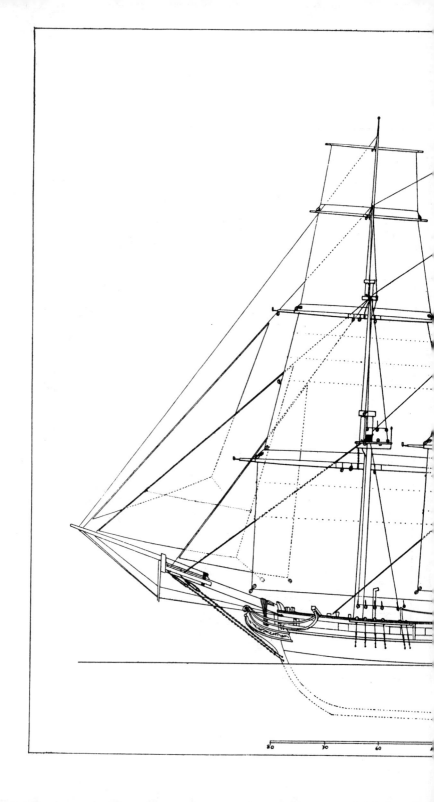

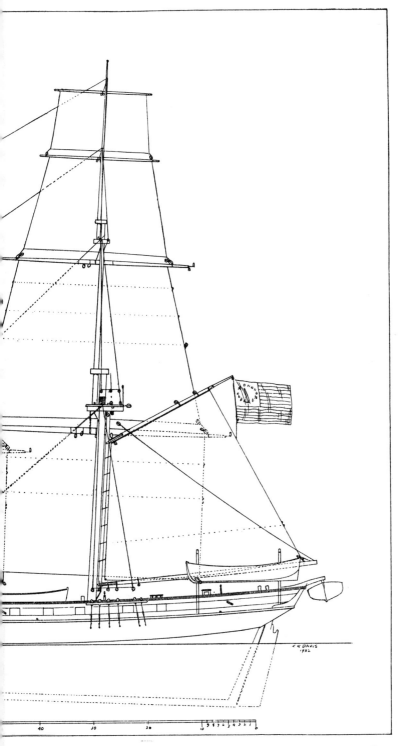

PLATE VI

VII. Beginning to Put up the Frames

VIII. The Hull Framed with Clamps, Bilge Strakes, etc., in Place

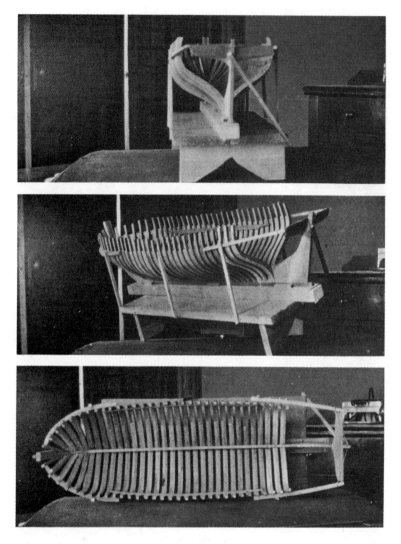

IX. Square Frames and Forward Cant Frames in Position

X. Rail Stringers and Rail in Place

XI. Spiling Being Taken to Determine the Shape the Upper Edge of the Sheer Strake will take to Fit it on the Model. Spiling Staff Shown

XII. Framed Complete, with Deck Clamps in

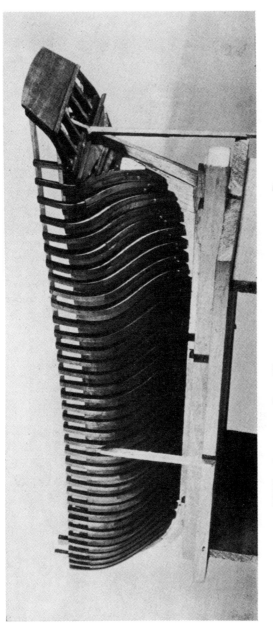

XIII. SHOWING ONE TIMBERHEAD CARRIED UP FOR BULWARKS

XIV. Hatch Coamings and Fitting-blocks between Beams for Masts in Place

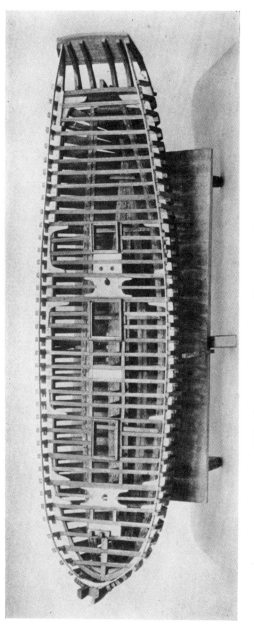

XV. Showing how the Deck was Framed

XVI. Center strip of Decking and Hatch Coamings in Place

XVII. SIDE VIEW SHOWING THE MODEL PARTLY PLANKED AND FIGUREHEAD IN PLACE

XVIII. Quartering Stern View showing Transom Construction

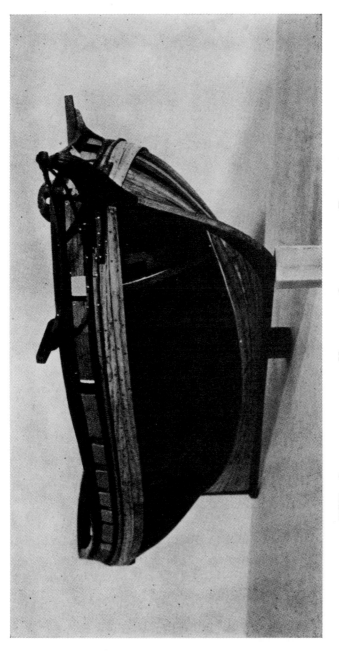

XIX. Showing how the Headrails Support the Figurehead

XX. Side View showing the Deck Fittings Completed

XXI. Quartering Bow View of Completed Model

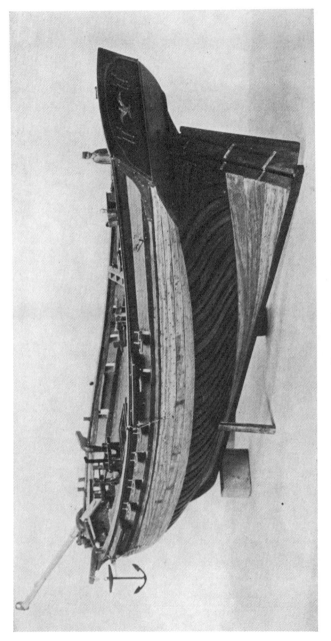

XXII. Quartering Stern View of Completed Model

XXIII. Mould Loft Floor showing Patterns for Frames

XXIV. Chopping Out a Hook-Scarph

XXV. Adzing off the Face of a Scarph after it has been
Sawed and Hewed

XXVI. Bevel Cutting Jig Saw for Cutting Futtocks of Frames

XXVII. How Frame Futtocks are Assembled on the Framing Platform

XXVIII. LIFTING A MIDSHIP FRAME WITH STEAM TRAVELING
GANTRY CRANES

XXIX.   Bow Frames Set Up in Place on the Keel

XXX. The After Frames Set Up and the Rudder at the Side

XXXI. British Brig-of-War of 1765

XXXII. UNITED STATES BRIG-OF-WAR, 1800

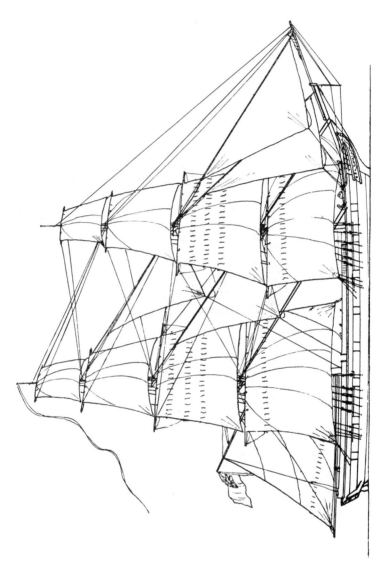

XXXIII. British 16-Gun Brig "Snake"

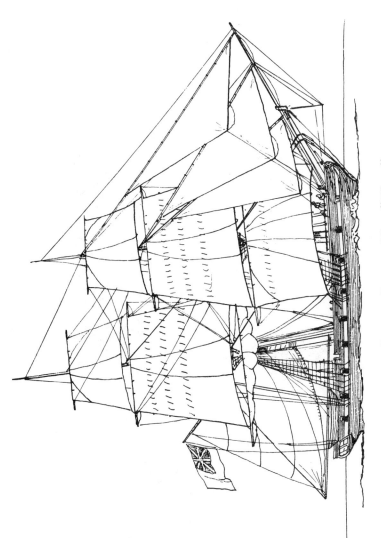

XXXIV. British Brig-of-War "Wolf"

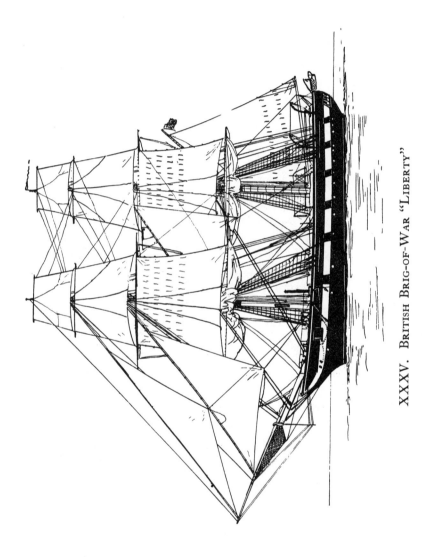

XXXV. BRITISH BRIG-OF-WAR "LIBERTY"

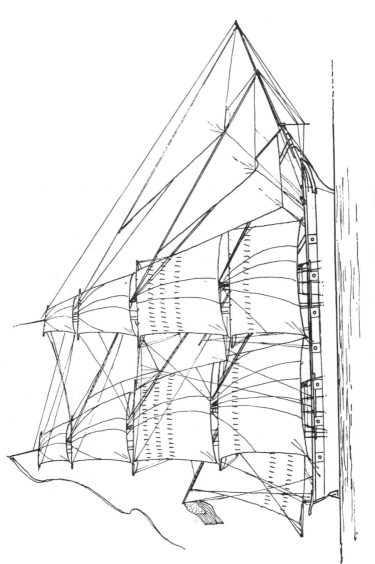

XXXVI. United States Brig-of-War

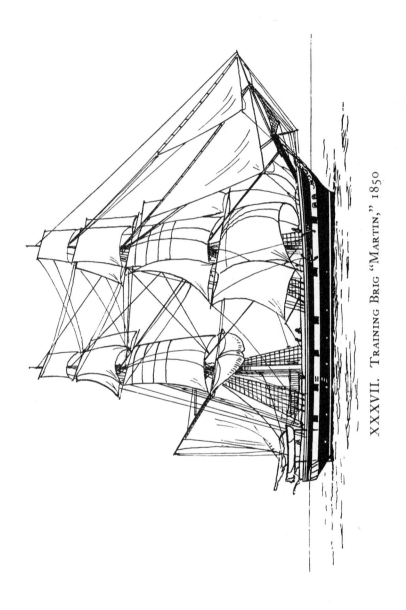

XXXVII. Training Brig "Martin," 1850

THE
BUILT-UP SHIP MODEL

THE
BUILT-UP SHIP MODEL

THE language of the sea and the men who have to do with the building of ships, is so full of strange names and technicalities, totally unintelligible to the layman, that many writers on nautical matters pass up all such as so much Chinese or Arabic; and the result has been misleading statements such as that it is only we, of this twentieth century, who have gone carefully into calculating and planning out our ships before building them. The public at large has been led to believe that the best they ever did in the eighteenth century was to whittle out a block model and saw it into sections to get the shape of enough frames to determine the ship's shape, or, to unscrew the horizontal lifts, or layers, of wood, the model was made of, and so plot the shape of the frames.

If one will but take the time to investigate this subject, and educate himself sufficiently in the study of naval architecture to comprehend what is written in some of the really wonderful books that have been published in the 1700's, he will find that the old shipbuilders made as many calculations and plans then as they do now. In those days the nation's greatest scientists were ordered by the king to study the subject, in order to make every test of the ships that could be made. They even went to sea on the ships to study their subject at first hand and all sorts of experiments were made not only in England but in France, Holland and Sweden.

There were, of course, men at that time, just as there are now, who built by "rule of thumb" methods.

3

Men who built from crude models and even from no model at all. They simply framed the ship to suit the eye. Such men left no records by which their work might, in later years, be reproduced; but the men who planned their work have fortunately left us much information, both on big ships and sometimes on small craft.

This makes it possible for us to now build up small replicas of their ships from the shape of those ships which have been printed in books of plans, or whose measurements are given in tables of offsets. Where the man of today gets confused is when he tries to figure out, piece by piece, how these ships were built, as this phase of the subject, except in a few cases, has not been preserved in its entirety. Some few plans, such as the framing plan, or a deck plan, are shown, but the hundred and one knotty points that come up are not explained. It is like having bricks to build a house, but no mortar. In this work we will try to supply the mortar so that the bricks will not fall down for want of something to hold them together.

No one historian has given us all the data and it is only by reading the works of many of them and compiling the rules of old-time shipbuilding, that we have found the required information. Take the subject of fastenings, as an example, a most vital part of ship construction, and try to find any definite rule to go by. It was part of the shipwright's education to know how many iron spikes and how many treenails were to be put into each piece of wood; how many drift bolts and how many clinched bolts each different joint required and of what size. What then was common knowledge among all associated with shipping matters, was not considered worth treating on. The sizes of the various timbers and the more intricate problems of how to lay out and cut the shape of cant timbers, wing transoms, hair bracket rails, harpin moulds, etc., we find treated at great length, as they were problems in geometric projection on which authors loved to air their knowledge. In my youth I had a peculiar position where I had a chance to observe this. I was apprenticed to study naval architecture under a man fresh from a naval college, just starting in business, where everything was higher mathematics. I listened to him all day and then went home at night to where my future father-in-law, a practical shipbuilder, was doing the actual wood cutting and fastening. This was a combination of theory and practice that would be hard to beat. I once spent a Sunday morning in a City Island mould loft, at a shipyard whose proprietor was demonstrating to my naval architect employer that the moulded edge of a transom took on the curve he said it did, in contradiction to the way the architects' plans had it drawn in,—and the practical man proved his point.

Now let us build a model of a ship, a real model, one that we and our descendants can look at with pride. Anyone who thinks such a model undeserving of this esteem has but to try his hand at it once and he will soon admit it is an undertaking. It is not like whittling a boat out of a block of wood. There you have something rigid, solid, something that will hold its shape, but in putting up a frame of a ship, piece by piece, you have the problem of keeping the whole structure straight and true. On a real ship a chalk line down the center, from stem to sternpost, gives you a line to drop plumb-bobs from and see that each frame is set up true, the frames being held by shores to the ground

and set up by wedges. On a model, a straight edge over
the top is the best means, as it leaves the frames all free
and clear so you can get at them and gives something
to which the frames can be temporarily braced, until
most of the frames are in when it may be removed.

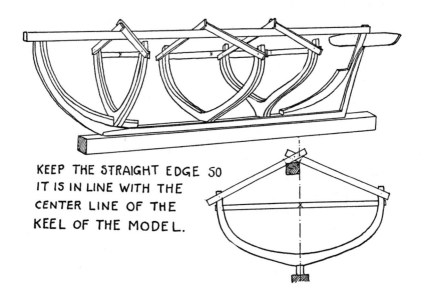

KEEP THE STRAIGHT EDGE SO
IT IS IN LINE WITH THE
CENTER LINE OF THE
KEEL OF THE MODEL.

Another method is to first set up at intervals along
the keel, temporary wooden moulds and then tack a
slat of wood down the center, fastened at bow and
stern, to hold them in place, one edge of the slat being
faired up to a straight edge and lined up on the center
marks made on each mould so as to be sure they all
set true in line as they must in order to make a fair
ship. Then around the outside of these moulds bend
small wooden battens, tacking them fast to each mould.
With these battens in place you will find it easier to set
up each set of frames as they are ready to go in and
you can visualize better the amount of bevel to which
each frame's edges, both inside and outside, must be

cut. Each frame should fit true against the battens, for if it does not do so, when it is put in it will have to be shaped off afterwards so that when the planking is put on it will lay in a fair surface, showing no bumps from forward to aft.

The moulds may be taken out when you have enough frames in to hold the boat's shape true, and frames may then be substituted in their place.

First of all, however, some base on which to build our ship must be provided, something that will hold its shape true and not warp. If we were only building a small vessel, a pine board as long as the model and as wide, with cross battens or cleats of wood screwed fast across it, underneath, at about four intervals to prevent its warping, would do and then down the center of this, on top, fasten a straight, square stick, about an inch square, on which to lay the keel.

So many model builders, when they first start in the game, try to build three-decked, one hundred and twenty gun line-of-battle ships, and nine-tenths of them fall by the wayside. That is a job that should be reserved until one has thoroughly mastered the art of shipbuilding, for the problem is much aggravated by the two additional gun decks. A single-decked vessel, like a frigate, is enough to stall many men, so we will first try our hand at one of these single deckers, a little brig-of-war called the *Lexington*, that was in America's first naval fleet fitted out at Philadelphia in 1775. In learning how to build her you can find out all that is necessary to build any single-decked ship, such as a frigate or sloop-of-war or a merchant ship. The only difference is in the plans you use to build from. The dimensions of the *Lexington* are: length on gun deck, 90 feet, 0 inches; length on keel, 76 feet, 5 inches;

beam, 22 feet, 8 inches; depth, 9 feet, 0 inches; tonnage, 166 tons.

The first step in making a built-up model after we have decided what ship we are going to build, is to get a set of plans of that ship to build by. Shipbuilding is an intricate job, far more so than any other kind of construction I know of, and wooden shipbuilding is worse than steel ship construction as the fastening of wood members is an art in itself. Wood shipyards had certain gangs of men trained to one class of work,—broad axe men, sawyers, plankers, framers, fasteners, —yes, and it even became so specialized in a certain section that in later years to bore a hole you had to send for one of the Wood Borers Association's men to do it. These men had all kinds of augers and specialized in nothing but boring holes. It may sound simple enough to bore a hole but if you have ever bored by hand keelson bolt holes through four, five and six feet of oak you will know that it is an art to do so and not have your auger "run" and become jammed.

But to return to our plans; if we were given a set of ship plans, showing her shape and her lines; and another set showing her construction, her spar plan, rigging plan and a sail plan, are we ready to begin and build her or not? The answer is *no*. To cut wood we have to lay those plans out, full size on a clean board floor, or mould loft, as it is called, and interpolate all the frames between the few shown in most plans. In a mould loft they make the full-sized patterns or moulds of thin wood, ½ inch or ¾ inch stuff, of every piece of wood that goes into the ship. These go out to the shipyard and there the sawyer gang lays the patterns out on the timber, marks out the shape by cutting a small grooved mark, with a race knife, all around the edges of the pattern on the timber and then the sawyer gang saws it out to that shape and gives it to the shipbuilders. This is comparatively simple, because it is merely cut out, square-edged, to the shape given. But suppose it is part of a frame in the ends of the ship. There, instead of the edges being sawed out square, they take a bevel, as they all do, and that bevel is not

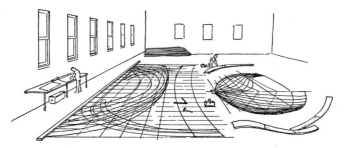

SHIP LAID DOWN ON MOULD LOFT FLOOR

the same all the way. That is where complications arise. The men in the mould loft, when they get out a pattern for frames, and it takes eight or ten separate pieces to make one frame, have to mark on the pattern the number of degrees the edge is to be beveled, or mark the angle itself on a small board that goes with the pattern. It may be six degrees at one end and diminish gradually to four degrees at the other end. To cut this the saws are made to tilt from the vertical, being operated by a screw gear, by hand, and can gradually change their angle while cutting. Without laying down the full-sized plans it would be impossible to find out how much bevel there would be. That is why we cannot build a wooden ship from just an ordinary set of plans.

Another point is that all the frames are not drawn out and to cut timber it is necessary to have some definite shape,—a pattern, to cut to. So if our plans do not show the shape of every frame or every other frame, at the least, we must draw them out. So I have taken the ordinary plans (lines and sail plan) and drawn out all the other plans necessary to build from. This is what every shipyard has to do in its mould loft. They have to "LAY THE SHIP DOWN," as it is technically termed, but which is nothing other than drawing her plans out, full size, on a clean, white painted, or clean, wood floor.

Every section which shows the boat's shape, if she were sawed in two at that point, has to be plotted out; not an intricate job, by any means, but a tedious one. The lines, as shown in the plan, are reproduced full size and to facilitate this the naval architect measures off from the paper plans in his office, as accurately as a small scale drawing can be measured, the widths from the center line of the ship to the side and the heights of each line in the sheer plan, measured up from a given base line,—a straight line,—at each given section; the forward perpendicular at the bow; the after perpendicular at the stern transom (the distance between these two representing her official custom house measurement for length); the midship or dead-flat; and the various other vertical sections; and writes all these measurements down in what is called a TABLE OF OFFSET, which is simply these measurements tabulated for convenience. One has to have some system about his work and the men who have to do this kind of work have found it convenient to neatly tabulate the measurements of each section under its given number or letter. You, building only one ship, may do it any way you like. You can take each section and treat it by itself, making a list of its widths from the center line and its heights from the base line, so long as you can reproduce the curve of that section; that is the ultimate object.

These sections are merely a means of reproducing the other curves, the waterlines and the buttock lines. These are as battens drawn from end to end of the ship

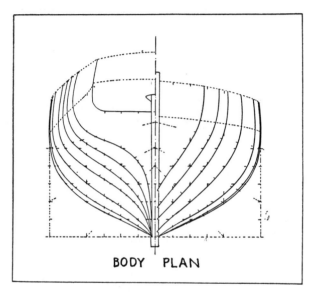

BODY   PLAN

and show how the surface curves along that line. Great care must be taken, in fairing up these lines, to see that the widths in the plan of the waterlines agree with the width in the corresponding spot in the sections. Give and take, on one or the other, until they do correspond and your eye will detect the one that makes an unfair curved line.

The diagonal lines x, y and z are run just as you would run battens around the frames and give more accurate results than crossing the sections at what more nearly approximates a right-angle intersection or an oblique crossing at some of the waterlines or buttock lines.

The enlarging of the small plan to the full size of the ship, magnifies any slight variation in measurement so that it is in this laying down process the ship's accurate form is obtained, a fair form to build up. When we have the form of the ship thus accurately delineated, we are ready to proceed with a construction plan and to lay out the thickness of the various timbers in their proper relation one with another. I have done all this for you in Plate No. 3 which shows just how our little brig was put together, and by referring to the photograph of the actual, here reproduced, you can get a pretty clear idea of how it is done.

You must understand at the outset that this is not to be a technical treatise on naval architecture. I will not lead you into deep water but try to show by description and sketches how such timbers as cant frames are put in, and how transom frames are shaped out, and do this without going through pages of projection and technical explanations such as may be found in Steele's "Naval Architecture." I'll try to find a shallow ford where you may wade across and get around this deep water.

Another gap in the necessary information to build, that generally confronts the model shipbuilder, is the question as to how big the various members of a ship's hull should be. Many plans do not give this information which was in the shipbuilder's private notebook. Some of the old descriptions of clipper ships published in the newspapers at the time when they were launched, contain detailed descriptions of their construction, for that was valuable news in the 1850's. Some old works on shipbuilding also give the sizes of all the timbers used in various classes of ships. The "American Lloyds" and the "American Bureau of Shipping," issued books of rules for determining the sizes of various ships timbers, and Samuel H. Pook, naval constructor in the days of sail, has given us condensed rules for determining the size of scantling for ships of war, all being a percentage of the ship's breadth of beam. He also gives the rules for figuring the size of all iron fastenings and much ships' ironwork, such as the chain plates, rudder pintles, etc. These will be found in the Appendix, and by using these rules we may determine, if our plans do not give them to us, the size of scantling for the model we are going to build.

It is the question of fastenings that influences the size of built-up models, because if you try to build on any scale under one-quarter inch you cannot get small enough fastenings. They would be so minute you could not even pick them up, except with a pair of tweezers, and good fastenings are as essential in a model as in a real ship, to hold it together.

Let us take the little 16-gun brig *Lexington*, of Revolutionary fame, and make a ⅜-inch scaled model as nearly like her as we can. With her plans here given, reconstructed as nearly as may be, we have but the beginning. We have her outline in sheer view, and deck plan or half breadth, and 14 sections of her moulded shape at the marked intervals along her length (Plate Nos. 1 and 2). These sections are spaced so they coincide with some of the actual frames; therefore we have the shape of a few of them. The frames are set up on the keel, in a spacing of two feet, frame to frame. The midship section marked *x* coincides with frame No. 17. All the other full frames space off every two feet along on the keel. Rule lines vertically, representing them, across both the sheer and the half-breadth plan and plot their shape between those few frames already drawn in as sections. This is not done ordinarily in a small plan drawing, as so many lines would come too close together to be able to identify any particular one; but now we must have each one individually, if we are going to build her. (See the plate where I have so drawn out all the frames that set square across the keel frames No. 5 to No. 33.) In Plate No. 4 (the midship section) all the various members of the ship's construction are designated so you may the better visualize the ship as a whole.

There is another way of doing this framing, if you are handy at making models and don't mind spoiling a few frames in practice until you get the knack of how it is done, and that is the way my son and I jointly made the model that is here photographed. He wanted to learn the whole process of shipbuilding so I first showed him how each piece of timber went into one of those Ferris type, wooden, 2500-ton steamships of which we were building ten, during the World War, eight of which, complete with machinery, we delivered from the Traylor Shipbuilding Corporation, at Cornwall, Penn. After completely framing this ship my son wanted to build a sailing ship model and we began on the *Lexington*.

The method I spoke of was to cut out of cigar-box wood five temporary moulds, as shown in the photograph, and around these he bent, on each side, five small battens which gave him a sort of skeleton outline to hold his frames in place in the ship as he sawed them out and assembled them. (See illustration on page 6.) Having sawed one, he could, with this skeleton mould before him, saw the next frame without reference to the drawing to determine its bevel. This is actually done in building some of the smaller types of coastwise craft. It is called "framed on ribbands," as ribbands and battens mean the same thing in shipbuilding language, a batten being a small one and a ribband a larger strip of lumber. Unless you have a keen eye for fairness, in sighting the curves, you had better stick to the safer method of sawing each frame to its shape as taken from the plans. But let me here warn you of the most common mistake of amateur shipbuilders, and that is, they work only to get the outside surface of their frames fair and true and neglect the inside. Now the inside is just as important, *if not even more so*, as the outside, for all the frames must be fair and cut to the proper bevels, because the inside fore and aft members of a ship's frame, such as clamps and stringers, are just as important as the frames themselves, to produce a fair shaped hull, and you will think even more so when you come to try to put them in.

You will find it much more difficult to cut out and fair up inside the hollows than you will to file off the more accessible rounded surface of the outside of the frame on a model. So work to make the inside of your model ship's frame fair in a fore and aft line from keel to deck clamp—every inch of it. Be careful to keep them all the same thickness or moulded depth and not have one too full and the next too scant, and have the same taper in their thickness, which decreases as you go up to the head or top of the frame.

The keel is naturally the first piece of wood to go into our ship, and here comes a question: what kind of wood are we going to use in building this craft? The old British admiralty models were always made of boxwood and so it is every model builder's ambition to make theirs of this wood. But unless you get bone dry, seasoned wood you will have trouble with it in curling and warping out of shape, and this is true of any wood — it must be dry, well-seasoned stock.

It was only because I had an opportunity to buy some seasoned black walnut that I decided to use that wood in the *Lexington* hull which my son Theodore built. He started it March 8, 1924 (we keep a time book on each model to see how many working hours each one takes to build) and June 2, 1925, had it all in frame with clamps, bilge stringers and keelson, in a working time of 138 hours. It was then put in the attic where it lay until November 5, 1931. When I brought it down again it stood as true and fair as the day it was put away with a coat of linseed oil, the only protection it had been given. Of course six years is a short time when compared with the two hundred years some of the older models have survived. I have seen a boxwood model so destroyed by some worm, ant or bug that had gotten into it, down in the tropics, they said, that it was a paper-thin shell only. It was one of Mr. H. H. Rogers' famous collection of models and I had it in my house for about a month to take off its lines and draw up a set of plans, details and all, so they could take it apart and using new wood where necessary, restore her to a sound condition. This is what happened. Every day the table top on which the model rested, had the outline of the ship marked in a very fine deposit of wood dust, where she was decaying. Fumigation and other attempts to kill the destroyers in the wood all had failed.

Now whether you decide to use a white pine keel, an oak one, a black walnut, lancewood, or De Gama wood, is for you to choose; its size for use in our model of *Lexington* is ¼ x ⅜ x 24 inches.

The sternpost is a simple affair, in such a craft as

ours, as the rudder is hung like a barn door, on the after edge of it, in a straight line. As it swings from side to side, at the top it requires a larger hole to swing in than the more modern "plug stock rudder," as it is termed, which is a round-headed rudder working in a neat-fitting, round hole, centered over the center of the pintles, leaving no space for water to squirt through at the stern.

Leaving the rudder until later, let us go on with the sternpost. Its shape and size is shown in the plan being the same thickness as the keel, ¼ inch. While in the real ship this is a separate timber and the deadwood forward of it, to which it is attached, is made up of one timber piled up on top of another until the area required is filled in and then all are bolted through and through or driftbolted, one on top of another, in our model,

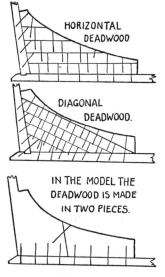

HORIZONTAL DEADWOOD

DIAGONAL DEADWOOD.

IN THE MODEL THE DEADWOOD IS MADE IN TWO PIECES.

we can simplify this by making the rudderpost and part of the deadwood all in one piece. Take a piece of ¼-inch thick walnut and saw out the shape as indicated in the plan and then cut another piece to complete the after deadwood. It is in making the long borings in such places as this deadwood, when we would send to the Wood Borers Association, if we were down in a Maryland shipyard.

Don't be in a hurry and crowd your drill when you bore holes here or you may experience trouble yourself and find the drill point breaking through the side of the deadwood. Press lightly and clear the drill of cuttings by drawing it out occasionally.

The stem and forward deadwood can be treated in the same way. Trace out the curved outline on the wood it is to be cut from and saw to shape. Be extra careful to see that the edges of the deadwood, stem and stern, are cut and finished exactly square so that when the keel is level, athwartships, the two will stand perfectly plumb, and not discover one sticking off at one side and the other out the opposite side. If they are not both standing perfectly plumb you have made a poor joint and your ship will be lopsided.

Before setting up either, see that the rabbet line is traced on them as that is where the planking is to end and a notch to receive this planking, termed the rabbet, has to be cut. In a real shipyard the bevels at which the planking will come down off the frame onto the stem and deadwood, would all be plotted from the full-sized plans on the mould-loft floor and this rabbet, or notch, would be chiseled out before the stem was set up. If we have it marked out we can do it more safely afterwards by taking a small sample of the actual size planking we are going to use and cut and fit it right on the model after the outside is all faired off with a file. We did cut just a very shallow notch in making our brig model, because it was a more permanent way of marking it. But if you do so, don't cut it deep, for the angle of bevel will fool you.

You may have wondered why the deadwoods stop just where they do on the plans. Well, there is a good reason for it. We have no deadwood all along the keel, in the middle of the ship, because all the frames between these deadwoods are what are known as "full frames," that is, they go clear across the keel from side to side continuously, frames No. 5 to No. 33 inclusive. The frames where there is deadwood do not go across the ship continuous, but are made in halves, one half on each side of the deadwood, and they are called "half frames." They butt up against the deadwood being jogged or mortised in a couple of inches on the real ship, and are bolted to it and through and through to each other.

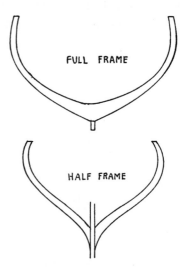

The reason these frames do not cross the keel is because at that point the shape of the ship's bottom has become so narrow and the frames make such an acute V, there is not room for the keelson to pass behind them without cutting down their strength; and as the keelson is more valuable from a structural point of view, forming as it does a truss with the keel below, than the frames, the keelson is allowed the preference. The frames by faying against the deadwood, so high, give ample room to fasten their lower ends to the deadwood, and the deadwood is a vital support to the stem and sternpost. The deadwood height is determined at that point where the inside edge of the frame meets it and can be measured off from the plans. Then again, in the two ends, the last few frames are not set square across the ship but have their upper ends swung forward of where their lower ends touch the deadwood. They are called "cant frames," because of the fact that they are canted, that is, turned, or inclined forward.

The same spacing is preserved at the deck, but the heels, the lower ends of the frames, all come close together like the leaves of a fan. By so doing, the extreme bevel, otherwise necessary, is greatly reduced, as the frames turn and face more squarely to the planking.

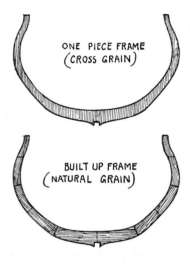

ONE PIECE FRAME (CROSS GRAIN)

BUILT UP FRAME (NATURAL GRAIN)

The frames in our model are all set square to the keel. She is built with her keel set level, fore and aft, and the frames plumb up from it. When launched she set by the stern, that is, her keel aft was deeper in the water than it was forward. Most old ships were so built, with frames squared to the keel, and the ship had to be built on an inclined set of ways so she could be slid down into the water when completed. In order to set the frames square to the keel, the same angle of inclination of the ways from the horizontal, was cut on a board, an "angle board," with a plumb-bob hanging down on the straight edge. In use, this angle board is held against the after side of a frame as it is being set on the keel and it is shored forward or aft until the plumb-bob hangs true along the straight edge of the angle. Occasionally this angle board is tried as a check to see that the frames are keeping the angle, but several frames are usually set up by measuring or using a spacing block between the frames to insure uniformity, after one is set by the angle board.

Before we take up the subject of cant frames let us complete all the midship part of our brig, between the deadwoods, where we have the easier to construct square frames, those that set square across the keel and go continuous across the boat.

It is evident if this frame is sawed out in one piece there is going to be some cross-grained wood in it, and that is why only boxwood is used in such framing, as no other wood would stand without

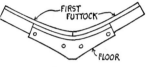

FLOOR AND
FIRST FUTTOCKS
IN POSITION

splitting, and even in using boxwood extreme care must be taken. The waste of this method is necessarily very great and even when done it is not "shipshape and Bristol fashion." A regularly built-up ship's frame is, to my mind, highly preferable as you have a model built

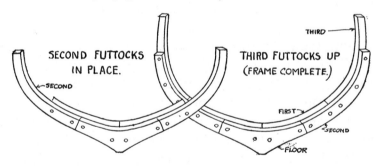

as the ship was built. The frame is far stronger for having no cross grain and the economy incalculably cheaper because you can use up every scrap of wood, and as to the time, if my son, who had never built but one model before, could frame the *Lexington* model as he did, put in keelson, transom timbers, clamps and stringers, as the accompanying illustration shows, and do it in 138 hours, it cannot be such a difficult job. This work extended over a period of 48 days with an average of less than three hours a day for that time.

This is the way she was framed. It is on the system Sir Robert Seppings introduced into the British navy. One half of the frame makes a floor timber that goes continuous across the keel and has an arm sticking out five or six feet on either side. The other half has two long, first futtocks that meet at the center of the keel and extend several feet above the ends of the floor timber. Then the second futtock, on each side, goes from the floor ends up to the deck and the third futtocks go from the end of the long, first futtocks to the rail forming the top-timber. So there are seven pieces in each frame; the floor timber and three futtock timbers on each side.

The frame is so carried up, futtock by futtock, each lapping the one on the other half — merely what would be called "breaking joints." Some would say we take two frames to make one and that perhaps expresses it clearer than any other statement. We do, but instead of making frames out of 16-inch oak (½ inch in the model) we make them of two 8-inch thicknesses (¼ inch in the model) and then shift the joints as shown, so that one half bolts or is treenailed, to the other half and the joints alternate, first one side then the other.

While this makes more pieces to keep track of, it's nothing so intricate but any man capable of making a model can work out systematically, by numbering each piece and finishing one frame at a time. Once you have caught on to the idea and worked out a frame by this, the regular shipyard system, you will not care to do it any other way. It has been my experience, so far, that to build and to rig a model and do it just as shipyards did, is the quickest and best way.

As the *Lexington* is built, each square frame is composed of seven pieces,—a floor futtock, and then a first

futtock that goes to the center of the floor futtock lapping it, and a second futtock and top-timber on each
side. Assemble these on a clean board on which is
marked a central line, a base line at right angles across
it, and on which either mark out the shape of each
frame, one at a time, as you make them, or, at least, the
extreme widths and heights so you can see that the
assembled pieces of frame come true. When assured on
that point glue the various pieces on all touching faces
and then fasten them with dowels, "treenails," it would
be, in the real ship. For this purpose you can buy a
package containing 72 dozen "Peerless Wood Applicators," made of white, hard wood, $6\frac{1}{2}$ inches long
and $\frac{3}{32}$ inches in diameter, for about 55 cents. These
drive snug in a hole bored with a number 46 drill.

The shape of the frame, as given in the plan, is the
middle of the frame, the seam where the two pieces
come together. And this brings us to perhaps the most
confusing part of getting out frames, the fact that the
futtocks on one side of this line, have to be cut with a
standing-bevel and the others with an under-bevel.
The reason for this will be made clear by the accompanying illustration. If the frame shape were taken at
the edge of a frame, the same bevel would answer for
both pieces, as if the frame were made of a single piece
of wood. But it has always been the practice in shipyards to do it the other way, and once you make up a
frame and figure out the bevel system, you also will
want to use it, as it is much more accurate.

By so doing, i.e., moulding to the center line, the two
adjoining edges, sawed to the same mould, will make
a fair frame, far better than if both futtocks are cut to
the same bevel, as by the latter method you will have
no definite line to set the second futtock against the

first and it will all become a matter of guesswork.

If you take time to number each futtock in a frame, as you cut them out, you will discover that all the even-numbered futtocks have one bevel and all odd-numbered ones have another; one a standing- and one an under-bevel, according to whether the frame be for the forward or after end of the ship. This will be a check against your sawing out a futtock to the wrong bevel. One or two mistakes of this kind are almost certain to occur and do even in real shipyards, but it will serve as a reminder to keep you going right on the rest of the futtocks composing a frame.

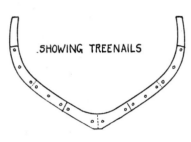

At each butt of one futtock to another, bore two holes, one in each futtock near the butt or end and one or two between butts so the holes are spaced about evenly along the frame, but closer at the butts. Dip an applicator in shellac or glue and drive it through each hole, cutting it off flush each time with the sides of the frame. Thus treenail the frame together, then, when you come to bore for plank or ceiling fastenings, you will not hit iron with your bitt as you would if nails or bolts were used instead of these wooden treenails. The treenails should just drive snug and if your applicators were good and dry they will stay in tight. It's a good plan to keep the box of applicators in a warm place for some time previous to using them. When running a wood shipyard, I had a room about twelve feet square, right back of the boiler room where it was quite warm, and cut out dowels by the hundreds and had them stacked up on open racks, drying, months before we needed them in ships, and when needed, only enough were taken out at a time for immediate use. Any left over were not allowed to lay out in the dampness of the night air but were returned to the drying room. Boys were detailed to do this work.

There is one frame in every ship that is cut with no bevel. It is at the widest part and is termed the "mid-

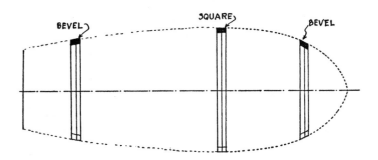

ship" or "dead-flat timber" and is located, in all old ships, a little forward of the ship's mid-length and marked with the symbol x. In our model of *Lexington*, this is 36 feet, 6 inches, aft of the forward perpendicular, or at the intersection of her main deck with the rabbet line at the stem. All the frames forward of this, owing to the shape of the ship as she narrows in forward, are beveled on the forward edge, and aft of it, on the after edge. While this bevel is imperceptible on the first few frames forward and aft of the dead-flat, it becomes very noticeable near the ends as you will soon discover when you come to saw them out. This is where the temporary moulds and batten method of framing will be of considerable assistance to you. By holding a piece of wood against the battens (or ribbands if it were a large ship) you can see about how much bevel there has to be cut on the face of the frame.

This can all be done easily in the case of a small model but in a real ship it is a "hoss of another color" and that is where the complexity of shipbuilding in reality begins to loom up. If I were to explain in detail to you the many steps that have to be gone through; how a tally has to be kept of each individual piece of wood that goes into a ship's frame; how each futtock has its varying size recorded and the bevels marked off on bevel boards showing the angle, the face, and back edge of each futtock of every frame to be cut; how, in the mould loft, all these bevels are obtained from the full-sized drawing of the ship's plans on the mould loft floor, you would quit in disgust. If there ever was a business that called for more concentrated attention, more patience, work and perseverance than does shipbuilding, never in over 60 years have I come across it, and you will find, even in building a small model, that you will need much the same qualities. Yet, piece by piece, it is simple enough. After all, what is it to determine bevels? If the boat widens out nine inches from frame number 11 to frame number 13, a distance of four feet, that gives you the angle of bevel at which the planking passes the intermediate frame number 12. It is an angle 48 inches on the base and nine inches on the perpendicular and that is all there is to it. All the mystery there is to it is in not getting confused; in doing it in a systematic manner; in taking the bevels on certain marked-in diagonal lines, such as *x*, *y* and *z* in our plan, diagonal as they cross the frames at as near as possible right angles, and then marking the same spot on the frames so the bevels will be sure to be cut where they were measured for. You can devise your own system so long as you understand the idea. Shipyards have found, for instance, that it pays to take off the bevels at points on the plan corresponding to where the ends of each series of futtocks come, as that gives them the bevels at each end, and, with maybe one more spot in mid-length, on any very long futtock, they have bevels sufficient to saw out that particular piece. If you are skillful enough you may judge the amount of bevel by your eye and jig saw your frame without measuring all the bevels.

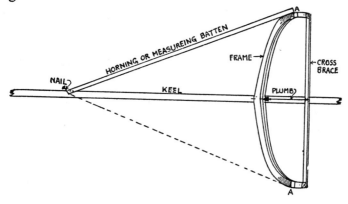

Set the midship frame up so its center is 36 feet, 6 inches aft of the rabbet, at stem, at the deck height, and the others, all two feet apart, center to center. In setting up the first frame with a straight-edged stay or brace tacked across it to hold it the proper width set exactly to the deck line, be careful to get it plumb, centered true by a center mark on the cross brace, or "cross spawl," to be nautical, plumb over the center line of her keel and squared by "horning it." This queer sounding term means nothing more than measuring with a stick, pivoted with a pin or nail, in the center of the stem head or sternpost and swung in an arc from side to side to see that both sides of the head of the frame are the same distance,—proof that the frame is setting square across the keel.

Don't get discouraged. It requires perseverance to build a good model, and I see by our time book that it took Teddy 64 hours to put up the 21 full frames, and then the model was laid aside from May 11, 1924, until Feb. 13, 1925, when he became ambitious and as it was no time of the year to go yacht racing, he tackled the model again and started putting in the cant frames, forward and aft, and when the total had reached just 100 hours, all the frames were in. With the battens

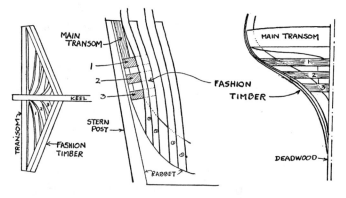

still in place, the bow frames, becoming straighter and straighter towards the bow, were very easily got out in two pieces, one for each half-frame with a half-frame flat against the stem, on either side, for knightheads, that lined up with the rabbet line. But aft, the opposite occurred. There, the frames became more and more crooked, more S-shaped and, as forward, a small brass screw was put through the heel or lower part of the frame into the deadwoods. The last frame, aft, was canted so it just came to the main transom's end. This frame is called the "fashion timber."

From the last frame, aft, to the rabbet on the stern-post, there is a blank space which has to be filled in with wood to have something to nail the ends of the planking to. This is done by horizontal pieces called "transom frames." They are horizontal and bolt to the sternpost in the center and their outer ends fit against and are treenailed to the after side of the last frame, this "fashion timber." The little triangle left below the lower transom is small enough to be faired out with a solid chock of wood treenailed fast against the dead-

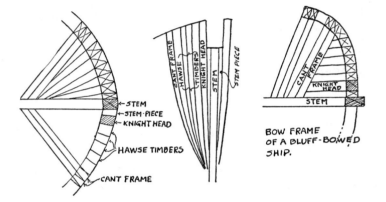

wood. Our little ship has only three lower transoms but some of the big line-of-battle ships had as many as eight or nine of them.

At the bow a somewhat similar method is employed to fill out the shape of the ship with wood for the outside planking to fasten to, only here, instead of horizontal pieces, vertical ones, "packing pieces," are used to fill in between the cant frames. The stem, not being as thick as the bowsprit of the ship, is padded out with a long, tapered piece on each side so their combined width at the top is equal to the bowsprit's diameter. These are called the "stem-pieces." Fitted against them are two long, stout frames called the "knightheads," that steady the bowsprit, sideways extending up above the main rail and sometimes having an ornamented head. They are bolted through the stem to each other. Outside of these is a solid pack made up of two or three frames bolted together and to the knightheads, but precaution is taken in their case to see that no iron comes where it will interfere in cutting through the hawse

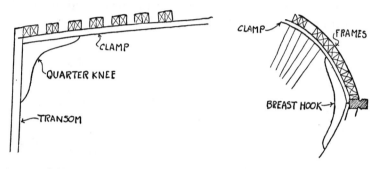

holes. The rest of the frames of the bow are just plain cant frames.

In some of the very bluff-bowed ships, there wasn't room along on the deadwood to get in frames enough without cutting down, too much, the siding, or width, of the frames. It used to be the custom to run as many cants as would work in readily and then fill in the remaining segment at the bow with frames set fore and aft with their heels bolted to the last cant frame.

Perhaps the best way for you to frame the cant timbers or frames in the ends, is by the use of the battens, "harpin moulds" they call them in the real ship, bent in a fair curve around the square frames and carried forward and aft to the rabbet in the bow and stern. By bending three or four of these you can be assured of a fair form on which to fasten the outside planking when you come to that part of the work, and by fitting in a thin board, cut to the shape of section No. *M* or No. *O*, even if only temporarily, you can be sure these battens are so bent as to give your ship the shape desired at that point.

In building a real ship, even though they go to all the trouble of projecting the shape of the cant frames to be sure they have the proper shape and bevel, they used to do, in a way, just what I have suggested you do. Instead of bending the shape with a batten, they sawed out the desired curve in what is termed a "harpin mould," a shaped-batten bolted to the last frame or two and the other end to the stem or, if it is aft, to the sternpost. You can easily do this by shaping a piece of thin board to the curves shown in the diagonal lines *X*, *Y* and *Z* and fastening it in place, taking care how-

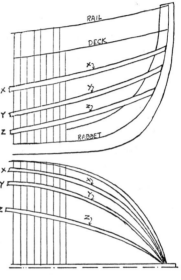

ever to get the cant frames set at the same angle the diagonals are drawn to in the plans. This will insure your getting the ship's shape in the ends exactly like the lines drawn in the plans.

The main transom bolts to the sternpost, its top edge cut with the crown of the deck beam, and it extends down to the tuck where the bottom plank, as the buttock lines show, comes to one point at the after perpendicular, as shown in the sheer plan. With the transoms in and all the bow timbers in place our craft now looks like a rowboat, and we are ready to stiffen up and pull all these frames into a fair line on the inside by putting in the fore and aft members, which are just as much a part of the ship's frame as are the ribs or frames. They consist of the keelson, limber strakes, bilge clamps, deck clamps, and shelves. The keelson is a piece of the same size as the keel, to be fitted directly over the keel on top of the floor frames and fairing out on the dead-woods at the forward end and butting against the dead-wood aft. In our model this is a piece of mahogany, $15\frac{1}{2}$ inches long, $\frac{1}{4}$-inch thick and $\frac{3}{8}$-inch deep, up and down. Then directly on top of this, a second piece, of the same size, called a "rider keelson," $19\frac{1}{4}$ inches long, extends onto both forward and after deadwoods. The lower keelson was fastened by a slim brad, into every other floor, going clear down into the keel, and the upper or "rider," was fastened by the same sized brads down through the floor timbers.

Before we can put in the deck clamps we have some careful measuring to do. The height of the main deck at the side must be marked at intervals on the frames of our model, in order to determine where the top edge of the clamp shall go. As it goes under the deck beams we have to determine the total thickness of the deck and the deck beams. The deck is three inches thick and the beams $9\frac{1}{2}$ inches deep; so measure up from the base line to the deck line, at the side, as drawn in the plan and transfer a series of measurements inside the frame to guide you in placing the clamps. These clamps are very important members in the ship's inner frame, and had best be got out of $\frac{1}{8}$-inch thick white oak, $\frac{3}{8}$-inch wide. They can be in one piece, from stem to stern. Taper the bow end, where it has to take quite a quick bend, to a little more than half its thickness, a full $\frac{1}{16}$ inch, and then stick that end into the steaming end of a tea kettle nozzle, to soften it and make it less liable to break. Pull it up snug to the inside of the frames, all high spots having been previously cut down, so it will bend in fair, and boring with a small drill, for each fastening, drive in a small brad; one brad in the after futtock of a frame near the top edge of the clamp, and one into the forward futtock near the lower edge. Do this at every frame, clear back to where the clamp is fitted snug against the transom. Work a second clamp strake of oak directly beneath the first one. This may be in two lengths with a joint amidships.

The clamp and transom are tied together, in the corners, aft, by oak knees, $\frac{5}{16}$ inch in thickness, with arms about two inches long, fastened with three long, slender brads in each arm through clamps into the frames and into the transom. These are the "quarter lodge knees." All knees laid horizontally, in this manner, are termed "lodge knees." Those set vertically being called "hanging knees" and where, as they sometimes do in ship construction, they are set diagonally, down from under a beam, they are known as "dagger knees." Big battleships often have their main deck beams, under the heavy guns, so reënforced with a hanging knee in the center and a dagger knee off each side.

Up in the bow, another knee, opened so wide between the arms that it is known as a "hook," is fitted in to tie the two sides of the clamp together and fasten to the stem. This "breast hook," set horizontally, should also be about $\frac{5}{16}$-inch thick and extend $1\frac{1}{2}$ inches on either side. This can readily be cut out of straight-grained wood, but the quarter lodge knees, if cut from such stock, should have the grain running diagonally from arm end to arm end, so that each will share in the cross grain, that is, unless you get forked branches from some tree and cut out natural crook knees, where the grain follows the shape of the wood as cut out into the form of a knee.

An oak bilge-clamp is then run in on each side, the same way, only this is white oak, ¼-inch square, tapered on the bottom a short distance at the bow end, where it is only ⅛-inch thick. It starts at one side of the stem, close up under the clamps you have just put in, and sweeps down so it goes about midway throughout the length of the boat, between the deck clamp and keelson. Below this, and tight against it, fit a ⅛-inch by 3⅜-inch piece of white pine, using small brads to fasten it, two fastenings at each frame, one into each futtock, staggered (that is, one near each edge of the piece being put in).

The shipbuilder's rule for driven fastenings (drift bolts) is that their total length should always be 2½ times the thickness of the piece they fasten. A 12-inch thick timber therefore should have bolts 30 inches long driven to hold it.

The brads you will find very useful in building this model, are a No. 20 brad, ⅜-inch and ½-inch in length. Some No. 18 brads will, when you come to put on planking, be found to drive with less danger of bending, but you will use two of the 20's to one of the 18's and may not be able to buy the No. 18. In a real ship, the whole interior is planked over between the clamp and bilge stringer and below the bilge stringer down to within one strake of the keelson. This last strake is called the "limber board" and is generally, in small vessels, left loose in short sections so it may be taken up to get at and clear dirt that may find its way into the ship's bottom and choke the pumps. It is not fastened, but the edge of the next strake, the "limber strake," should be chamfered on its lower or inner edge, so that the last, the limber board, in short, loose sections, will fit square against it as it lays diagonally up against the keelson.

Aft, at the transom, a knee on each side, nailed to the transom and to the first two frames through the clamps, tie the stern securely together. Forward, a knee called the "breast hook," crosses each side of the stem, on the lower deck clamp strake, and is fastened to stem and frames through the intervening clamp.

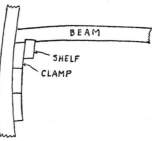

While a real ship has to be ceiled up inside to keep the cargo from laying in the bilge water between frames, we leave the little model un-ceiled so that the construction may be seen and the air allowed to have free ventilation to prevent dry rot.

To form a better landing for the many deck beams, another square piece of timber, known as the "shelf," is fitted around inside of the upper clamp and flush with the top of it, if anything, a little higher, so that the crown of the deck beams may be allowed for and the beams be sure to fit snug on both shelf and clamp.

Bore for all fastenings, especially any that go into hardwood, such as oak or black walnut. A little thumb vice is the handiest and chucks the small drills better than an "egg-beater" drill. When you drive a brad, always hold a heavy weight, such as a light flatiron or any handy chunk of iron you may have that can be held on the frame against which you are hammering, and use a very small hammer.

The "shelf" you may not be able to bend in, even by steaming it, as it takes a pretty sharp curve around the

bow. One way of accomplishing this part of the construction is to bend it in in two ⅛-inch thicknesses.
If you do, cut down the end of the ¼-inch part that
runs from the stern knee, aft to where it begins to bend
sharply so the inner layer butts against it and the outer
⅛-inch layer laps back on the half of the shelf for
two frames. By doing so, both do not end at the same

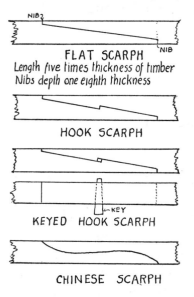

FLAT SCARPH
Length five times thickness of timber
Nibs depth one eighth thickness

HOOK SCARPH

KEYED HOOK SCARPH

CHINESE SCARPH

place, and make a weak
spot at the joint. Another
way is to cut the shape out
of a wide piece of wood.
First cut a paper pattern
that fits inside the frames
to the center of the stem
and then jig saw out a ¼-
inch piece which, after
you have made a perfect
fit and beveled it, you can
saw out the inner edge
leaving the desired ¼-inch
width for the clamp. In
doing this in our little
model, I made a butt joint,
the model being so much stronger proportionally than
the real ship. You can make this a scarph, if you like,
but observe the shipbuilder's rule if you do. Nothing looks so badly in a model as to see short scarphs,
only 2 to 2½ times the thickness of the timber being
scarphed. The shipbuilder's rule is no scarph should be
less in length than five times the thickness of the timber. That is a standard rule, exceptions only being made
in making it longer as is sometimes the case with the
keel where the scarphs should always span two frames
and receive the through bolts from the keelson that

go clear down through the frames and keel. Otherwise, if no special consideration has to be taken into account, always splice timbers with a five to one ratio of length to thickness.

There are two principal kinds of scarphs used in shipbuilding, the flat scarph and the hook scarph. In the flat scarph the two adjoining surfaces are flat, but never run them out to a shim edge. That is a grave sin never permitted in a shipyard as the shim ends rot away too quickly. The ends of the scarph should be $\frac{1}{8}$ the thickness of the wood, a square end that thick. Many flat scarphs were used in old ships but while they only showed the straight seam (and are therefore permissible in models representing old ships) if the scarph were opened up you

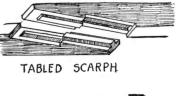

TABLED SCARPH

would find round coaks or short dowels embedded halfway, in each face of the scarph, that acted as keys, to prevent the two surfaces sliding and also formed a stop water for the bolts that were bored through them. Such scarphs were used mainly in putting timbers together to make deck beams.

The hook scarph, where the wood itself is hooked or locked together, is the old standby of the shipbuilder. The nib ends are $\frac{1}{8}$ of the timber in depth, the hook in the middle being $\frac{1}{8}$ also. A keyed scarph is made the same way but where the hook comes the two faces are left a little apart, slightly V-shaped in their horizontal opening, and into this V a hardwood wedge is driven home that jams the ends of the scarph snug, wood to wood. Hook scarphs or a type known as tabled scarph, used to be largely used in the heavy members of a ship's frame, such as in the keel, for it took from 11 to 13 pieces, spliced together by scarphs, put end to end, to make up the keel of a first-rate line-of-battle ship. This scarph was made the same as a hooked scarph save that one face of each piece had a tenon on its thin end, ⅓ its width and extending up 1½ inches, and on its thick face, a similar mortice was cut to receive the tenon on the other piece of the keel. When these two members were fitted together, the tenons going into the mortices, one had a true hooked scarph with considerable end-to-end wood bearing to resist being pulled apart lengthwise, even without the added security the bolts gave.

The ingenuity which some of our Far Eastern brothers display, in accomplishing the same end in a far simpler manner, was brought home strongly to me one day when I had an opportunity to see a Chinese scarph. There were no chiseled-out, square holes, each corner forming a starting point for a crack upon the least strain from any direction other than the endwise pull expected. In a Chinese scarph, only a wave-like, S-shaped cut united the two timbers, the whole surface of the wave forming a friction and effectively preventing the two pieces pulling apart lengthwise, if held together by bolts, as they were. To pull apart, the ends of the wave-shaped splice or scarph must ride up over each other, and such a scarph has no breakable corners.

Whatever is to be done below decks should be done now while the boat is wide open on top and easy to get at. A real vessel would now be ceiled up on the inside. The bottom, from the limber strake to the bilge strake, is ceiled up inside with heavy stuff,—"thick stuff," as it is technically called, 5½ to 6 inches thick, on a little craft like our brig, while the outside planking is only three inches thick. These thick strakes are run particularly in the turn of the bilge where they cross the joints in the frames at the floor futtocks, and are considered so important that they are hook scarphed together and have a through-bolt in each futtock end, riveted up inside. It is by such means that local weakness in one member is strengthened by another.

In models it is customary to leave off some of the ceiling and planking so as not to hide all the painstaking work that has gone into producing such a model, and also to show that it is not faked up or partly carved out of a solid piece of wood and only framed across where it is exposed to view, as is done in some cases.

The lower deck, or berth deck on a war craft, leaves so little room in the bilge or bottom of the ship, that in order to get at the water casks and provisions stowed below, the flooring was laid in the form of hatches or removable sections, in suitable lengths to permit handling readily. The after section, the steerage, ward room, and cabin, had permanent floors with scuttles giving access to the spirit room and magazine, and the bulkheads separating these rooms, were permanent. Part of this layout may be shown to advantage if one cares to go into that detail; but we will be satisfied in our case with the fitting in of the beams and maybe a part of the flooring that will not hide too much of the ship's construction.

We now come to where the real work of modeling begins. It's a good deal like the building of a house, for in a few days one sees, in a heretofore vacant lot, the skeleton framework of a building loom up. But although the entire frame is up, it may be a couple of months yet before it is ready for occupancy. And so, with a boat; while the complexity of a boat's frame makes it more difficult to erect, it, like the house frame, is but the beginning, though it shows up prominently. The hundred and one little points now arise and one soon begins to realize how little he really knows about ship construction. Take the next step that confronts us, for example, the framing of the stern of our brig. We must also realize that while up in Maine they might frame it by transom and top-timbers, boxed into and bolted to the transom set in a fore and aft line, except the quarter timber at the corner which will take a rake according to the shape of the desired transom; down in a southern shipyard they might frame it entirely differently by swinging a set of cant timbers or fan-like frames, one set fore and aft alongside the stern-post with the knuckle-shaped timbers necessary to give the shaped stern required and spread far enough apart at the head to make the proper rudderport, the next one swung a little farther from the true fore-and-aft line of the ship and the next a little more so, and so on until the stern is framed. The corner timber will be, as I said before, a different rake as it has to mate with the tumble home of the topsides and yet harmonize with the rake of the transom.

Different nations had different ways, too, just as in New York shipyards there was a difference between a Webb-built ship's stern and a Brown and Bell stern. The former always framed his stern between the wing transom and upper counter into two, an upper and a lower counter or transom, as the average man would call it, the lower counter being just wide enough to house the rudderstock, the angle of the face of the two being slightly different, the upper counter more approaching the vertical, and forming a knuckle through the middle between these two. Brown and

Bell, on the other hand, would frame it as one surface and at one angle, a single counter stern.

There is a lot of ship character expressed in the con-
tour line of the stern and we
have in our little brig one
that was very popular during the early nineteenth century. The navy brigs and topsail schooners and sloops-of-
war of 1820 and thereabouts,
nearly all were so modeled,
as were the Baltimore clippers.

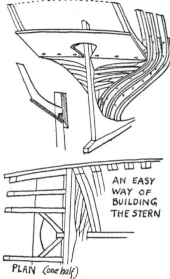

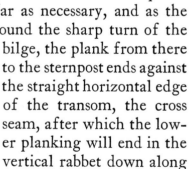

AN EASY
WAY OF
BUILDING
THE STERN

PLAN (one half)

If you have the stern
frame all in, transom frames,
and a wedge-shaped filling
piece below the lowest one
and aft of the last frame, you can see how the top side planking can run aft as far as necessary, and as the planking goes on down around the sharp turn of the

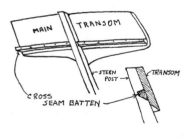

MAIN   TRANSOM

STERN POST

TRANSOM

CROSS SEAM BATTEN

bilge, the plank from there
to the sternpost ends against
the straight horizontal edge
of the transom, the cross
seam, after which the lower planking will end in the
vertical rabbet down along
the sternpost.

We begin to build our stern at this cross seam, by screw fastening or bradding on a batten, about ¼-inch square, keeping its lower edge ⅛-inch above the seam, and this edge must be beveled to match the angle that the counter makes with the sternpost. This gives us something to fasten the counter to. Then "we put the cart before the horse," so to speak. That is, instead of mortising a lot of small stern frames into this cross-

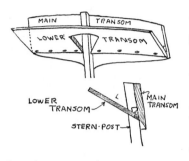

piece and building a skeleton framework of the whole stern, before planking it up, we start by cutting out a thin wooden pattern. I had some fine dry aeroplane mahogany, ⅛-inch thick, that I used. Cut this roughly to the shape and size required by the plan, but leave it well oversize so that you can cut down the edges afterwards. Clamp this up in place, after cutting out a slot to straddle the sternpost, and you have something to work on. Mark the center line on it, as should be done at all times, to keep the whole structure true. Saw out of ¼-inch thick piece of walnut, two knuckle-shaped frames, to the angle made by the upper transom and the counter, for the quarter timbers that, with their lower ends fitted against the batten at the cross seam, will fair up on each edge of

THE PROPER WAY TO FRAME STERN.

the counter with a batten or two run temporarily along the side back until it shows a true, fair curve. Fit the heel of these down against the transom frame, placing them both at equal distance from the center, and fasten them to the ⅛-inch thick mahogany counter and we have the beginning of a stern frame. Before it is fastened in place take a piece of wood, cut to the size of the rudderhead, and cut out an opening that will permit it to swing 45 degrees, as the rudder would swing each way, in the thin counter. Instead of using brads you will find No. 3 or No. 4 brass screws, ¼-inch long, with flat heads, are much better, as they draw the two parts of the work closer together. They are a smaller screw than most stores carry in stock but you can buy them. After you have the quarter timbers fastened on you can trim off the thin mahogany with a long file so that the sides fair up. But don't trim too much until you stiffen the counter

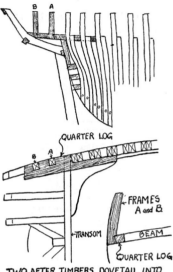

QUARTER LOG

FRAMES A and B

TRANSOM

BEAM

QUARTER LOG

TWO AFTER TIMBERS DOVETAIL INTO THE QUARTER LOG.

and quarter timbers by getting out a ¼-inch square piece cut on its upper edge with the crown of the deck and beveled to lay fair with the deck and fastened to

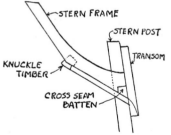

STERN FRAME

STERN POST

TRANSOM

KNUCKLE TIMBER

CROSS SEAM BATTEN

the top of the counter and butted against and bradded to the quarter timbers at the knuckle. This stern, when up, finishes off the after end of our ship most admirably.

The quarter log, another timber of ¼-inch stuff, ⅝-inch wide and 3 inches long, should be fitted so it lays fore and aft on top of the clamp away aft against the inside of the last two timberheads. Reduce it in width, enough to let it stick out aft of the last timberhead so it comes flush with the outside of the frames and beveled on the under side aft so it fays down on the quarter timber and by being bradded to it and to the clamp, on which it lays, it stiffens the stern frame. It also gives a nailing surface

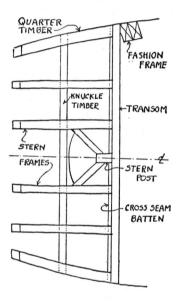

for the waist strakes when we come to put them on. And in the edge, by cutting a dove-tail mortice, another bulwark stanchion can be secured upright to match up with the other timber heads forward of it.

On the inside of the counter, fit two short fore-and-aft timbers on each side of the sternpost, with two others radiating from the sternpost, one each side of the hole cut for the rudderhead, to make that a sort of well to keep out any water that might find its way in if the canvas rudder coat should become torn.

The foregoing description of how to build the stem is a makeshift way and after I had it on and looked at it several days, I took it all off and framed it shipshape. This was done by cutting out four more stern frames to the same pattern as the knuckle or quarter timbers. Their heels, or lower ends, were notched over the batten and they fayed against the transom and were fastened to it by brads driven through from the forward side of the transom into the heels of these stern frames. Be careful to keep the two inner ones far enough apart to permit the rudder to swing 45 degrees each way.

At the toe, the lower tip of these stern frames, I nailed on each side of the sternpost to the transom a batten, beveled so its lower edge was square to the bottom plank and thick enough for the planking to butt against. Its upper edge was beveled so it was square with the plane of the lower transom.

Across the knuckle I then fitted a rabbeted piece of walnut $\frac{5}{16}$-inch square, with its top edge set square to the plane of the upper transom and its lower edge rabbeted so it would receive the planking of the lower transom square to its face. This knuckle timber I jogged at its ends, where it butted the quarter or knuckle frame on each side, so the rabbet came just flush. It served to keep the knuckle frames spread the proper distance and half of it ran past and across the after face of them to the outer edge of the knuckle frames to which they were bradded. The four intermediate stern frames, cut the same shape as the knuckle frames, were jogged out at the knuckle so their faces also came just flush with the rabbet in this knuckle timber, and each was bradded fast to it making a very rigid stern frame.

By this mode of framing we have made every provision for receiving the planking at both the cross seam and the knuckle, and it is more "shipshape" than putting on the plank first and then dummy frames as before described.

I have not attempted, in this model, to go into some little refinements that were considered very essential to make a handsome looking ship in later years, as in the days when these little brigs were built, during the Revolution, time was more essential than looks. The round given to the face of a ship's transom was to relieve the flat effect. The wing transom, instead of being a straight stick, was slightly curved so the ends at the fashion timber (frame), to which they fastened, were forward of the middle at the sternpost. And it was also given a slight curve downward on the outer ends. It is only necessary to so curve the wing transom if we want a sweep in the face of our transoms, preserving this same sweep and crown (like a deck beam) at the knuckle to get this effect, but our ship was not so built so we will build her with a flat transom.

In the open gap between the last short top-timber, the one we dovetailed in, and the knuckle frame, we fitted another short top-timber to have something to nail the waist strakes to. The

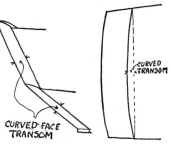

CURVED
TRANSOM

CURVED-FACE
TRANSOM

rail clamp being secured gave us something to fasten its top to, and its lower end set on the knuckle frame and was fastened by a brad driven from below. This timberhead was not in when I had the photograph taken of her deck frame, nor was her rudderport framed, nor the short pieces of beams between the stern frames, that gave support and a nailing surface for the deck planking that carried clear aft to meet the inside of the crosspiece the knuckle frames jogged over. To put in these sections of beam you can let the ends into the knuckle frames and stern frames.

The rudderport was formed by fitting in two diagonally placed pieces, one edge beveled so one end fays against the sternpost, flush with the deck beams, and the other ends against the knuckle frames, forming a 90 degree angle between their faces, so that the rudder may swing 45 degrees each side of the center line. One bolt (I took a piece of wire) can be put through both ends and the head of the sternpost, to hold the forward ends, and a brad in each of the after ends holds their beveled ends snug against the knuckle frames. Then I fitted a chock between the knuckle frames, that fitted against the knuckle batten aft and against these two pieces, fitted with an arc-shape cut out of its forward edge that just cleared the rudder as it swung or could swing on its pintles.

This necessitated making a rudder which I shaped according to the plan, out of $\frac{1}{4}$-inch black walnut. The post was made from a piece $1\frac{3}{16}$-inch wide and then a backing piece bolted on that was only $\frac{1}{8}$-inch wide at the top, which was rounded and stuck up $\frac{1}{4}$ inch above the stock piece where it was narrowed down to the $\frac{3}{8}$-inch width it carried up to the top. At its lower edge this backing was another $1\frac{3}{16}$ inch in width, making the rudder, at its widest part, $1\frac{5}{8}$ inches, the bottom edge cut parallel to the rabbet line. The rudder was tapered to $\frac{3}{16}$ inch in thickness at its lower end, on the post, the taper starting up about $4\frac{1}{2}$ inches from the bottom and it was $\frac{3}{16}$-inch thick at the top of the backing piece, tapered to $\frac{1}{8}$ inch at the lower after corner. The forward edge was chamfered off on each side 45 degrees, leaving $\frac{1}{16}$ inch of it square, down the center, from a point $6\frac{3}{4}$ inches up from the bottom edge where it came to the deck level. Above that it was left square edged. As soon as it was made I gave it, as with all new work, a coat of linseed oil.

In the so-called "plug stock" type of rudder, previously referred to, the rudderhead was a round stick where it went up through the hull of the ship, and the pintles and gudgeons, which formed the hinges upon which it turned, were placed in a line directly under the center of this round spar-like stock. Just outside the planking under the ship's counter, this round rudderhead was tapered down conically to a point that centered just above the uppermost pintle. This cone shape was complete on the forward side of the rudder but on the back it moulded into the flat of the rudder blade. This necessitated a gouged-out shape, in the top of the sternpost, to receive the projection of the rudderhead forward of the center line of the pintles and rudderhead.

The hole up through the ship's stern was not necessarily round. It was a box-like compartment with a round hole cut to fit it at the deck where it came up through the hull, and a piece of planking, termed the "pot lid," fitted below where it entered the hull. This "pot lid" was removable, for to unship this kind of a rudder, after raising it sufficiently to lift the pintles up out of the gudgeons, the rudder had to have room, in the rudderport, to move aft until the upper pintle was clear of its gudgeon so that the rudder could be lowered down and taken out of the ship. Many ships had a removable wooden collar fitted at the deck, by removing which, in two sections, more freedom was given the rudderhead to move aft and so reduce the amount the rudder had to be tilted aft to clear the top gudgeon. Some old-time ships, especially men-of-war, had a series of collars fastened to the rudderhead's top, with engaging collars that fitted into or under each, that carried the weight of the rudder and were kept well greased to insure easy turning and prevent chafing. This was done to prevent a sea from lifting the rudder when the ship was deep in the water and possibly unshipping it, and when unloaded, "flying light" in ballast, it took what would otherwise be a very heavy load off the gudgeons.

In the merchant service this was accomplished by means of a dumb brace and a wood lock. The dumb brace was a metal lug or shoulder bolted to the stern-post, just below a gudgeon, onto which the pintle set, after going through its gudgeon. This relieved the wear on all the other pintles and gudgeons and made it easier to turn the rudder. The wood lock consisted of a block of hard wood set into a cut-out in the forward edge of the rudder, close up under a pintle, to prevent its being lifted up and unshipping. It was wider on one side, the side it was fitted in from, the space cut out for it being so beveled and it was held in place by a bolt driven diagonally through it and the sternpost. With this block in place the rudder could not be unshipped, yet to remove it and unship the rudder, all that was required was to back out this one bolt which went clear through the sternpost and remove the block of hard wood called the "wood lock."

The frame of the deck next claims our attention. For that we go back to our plans and measure off the location of each mast, hatchway, bitt, etc. First put a square batten down the center of the model, laying it in against the stem and sternpost, and space off on this where the masts, etc., come. You can remove it as you work and it is always handy to put in to find where the next set of beams go.

First locate the heavy beams, one forward and one aft of each mast, and note what frames they come against. The beams butt against the frame, not alongside of it.

To make the beams, get some $\frac{1}{4}$-inch black walnut, the same kind of stock the whole frame was made of.

Mark out the shape of the beam, with its camber or crown, and cut a pattern out of stiff cardboard to use in marking out their shape preparatory to cutting.

The crown we are using in this brig is seven inches in 23 feet, that being a few inches short, maybe, of the length of the beams amidships. To lay out an arc, use any of the various methods shown in the accompanying diagrams. One way of insuring uniformity in the

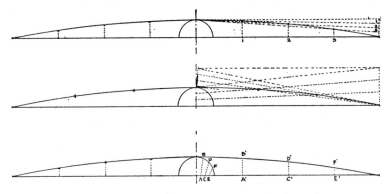

THREE WAYS OF LAYING OUT THE DECK BEAM CROWN.

beams is to get a thick piece of black walnut and saw out the shape of the beam and then rip it up into as many as it will make. It makes a far more natural looking ship model if you observe all the little niceties of construction and vary the width of your beams as was done in actual practice and not have every beam the same width. So for the main beams, the first ones to be put in, the beams afore and abaft each mast, at each end of the hatchways, at the forward bitts, and at each side of the captan, use beams $\frac{5}{16}$-inch wide and for the intermediate beams use $\frac{1}{4}$ inch.

About eight of these heavy beams are needed. Under each of these put a hanging knee and tie them securely to the side frame with lodge knees. Cut cardboard patterns until you have the proper angle and then jig saw these knees out of some close-grained wood, like apple or maple, that is not apt to crack when you put in the fastenings, for, unlike in a real ship, where natural, crooked-grain knees can be had in oak or hackmatack, we have to cut them, for our model, out of straight-grained stock. This may be avoided if we live in the country, as I do, where after every heavy wind storm I go out and gather up the maple branches that have been broken off in the fall of the year after the sap has left the tree tops. All kinds of crooks and forks may be cut from these branches, and then you have the strength of the natural grained wood.

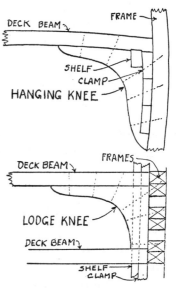

When you have the mast beams fitted, measure from the plan, where the center of each mast goes, and fit in the mast steps to receive the heel of the masts, before you fasten the beams.

There are several different ways of forming the mast steps. One way is to fork the lower end of the mast, banded with iron, just above the fork, to prevent its splitting, and let it straddle a V-shaped tenon cut by chamfering the edges of the keelson with stiffening floors across the keelson, forward and aft, out to the sides of the ship. But this fork or mortice, on the heel of the mast, is not considered so good or as strong as a tenon which steps into a mortice cut in a bed of oak to receive it. The crushing strain on the heel of a mast is tremendous and only the hardest, toughest kind of woods are used for the stepblock. The steps are set on

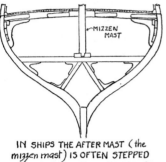

IN SHIPS THE AFTER MAST (the mizzen mast) IS OFTEN STEPPED ON THE LOWER DECK, OR ORLOP DECK, WITH BRACES BUILT IN UNDER IT.

the top of the keelson or backbone of the ship, except in the case of a ship where, as is often done, the mizzen mast is stepped on the orlop deck. In this case the orlop deck is stiffened by vertical and diagonal shoring of timber.

This practice of stepping the mizzen on the orlop deck has caused many a student of old shipping to make the mistake of setting the height of the mast as given in old documents from the keelson up, with the result that the mizzen appears very short as compared to the mainmast. One way of checking up on this point is to note where the top of the mizzenmast comes. It was the general custom to have the top of the mast come level with the mid-length of the mainmast head.

I took a block of black walnut, about ¾ inch in width and long enough to cross on top of the keelson and fit beveling against the limber strake. I slightly notched the under side of this piece to steady it athwartships on top of the keelson, and out of the top of this piece I cut a mortice ⁵⁄₁₆-inch long and ³⁄₁₆-inch wide, where the plan showed her mast was to come. With this in there was nothing to take our attention but the deck frame. So the mast beams can now be fastened in with very small brads. The mast or partner beams are two frame spaces apart. In the center where the hole is to be cut to permit the mast to go through, there is a solid pack of timber notched half way the depth of the beam and let in fore and aft to the depth of about two inches, just enough to steady it. This should be bolted together fore and aft through the beams.

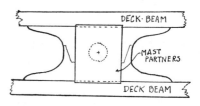

The mast partners should be as thick as the beams themselves. Outside of this partner, on each side, are to be fitted two knees, their fore and aft arms married together, that is scarphed one to the other. In our case, make a pattern of the space, out of cardboard, to represent these two knees and after marking out this shape on some quarter-inch pine, jig saw the knees out of one piece. It will look the same when in, but if you want to be particular, make two individual knees and scarph them together. If you do go to this extent of exactness, be sure to use either apple wood or maple wood. A most handy tool to do this fine fitting with is a small file. Get a set of what are called die-sinkers, files of a varied lot of shapes, square tapered, round tapered, flat, saw- or knife-shaped, round, half-round, etc. And while talking about it perhaps you have already found out that a 12- or 15-inch wood rasp is a most handy tool to use in fairing up pieces of wood, in place of a plane.

Fasten the ends of each beam with a brad down into

the shelf. Under the beams are to be fitted what are termed "hanging knees," that are to unite them to the frame of the ship. As before, fit a cardboard pattern to the shape you want this knee and cut it out of natural crooks. It seems a far cry to cut out a knee from a crooked piece of a tree branch. But when you have done it, just as the shipbuilder did it in days gone by, you will be glad you took the pains, not only for the natural, shippy look it gives to the model, but for the fact that when you come to put in the fastenings you will have the satisfaction of knowing that it is not going to split into two pieces just as you have it about done; and as for strength, there is no comparison.

At first I tried a knee cut out of straight-grained wood and had the whole lower end crack off after it was all in and I gave it one more tap to tighten it up snug. The result was that I put on my hat and went out to vacant lots in search of tree prunings. I found a lot of branches and with a small saw proceeded to cut off every crook where a branch made about a right angle with the main limb. They were all small branches, nothing bigger than an inch or inch and a half in diameter, with the off-shooting twig $\frac{1}{2}$-inch in diameter. With my jackknife I slabbed off the bark on one side of one of them, marked out the shape of my knee, and jig sawed and cut out the shape desired; then, with a saw, slabbed the knee into the thicknesses I wanted and I had as pretty a ship knee (in miniature) as ever went into a ship, and it was all done shipshape. It was notched out around the shelf and clamped to a neat fit, then marked where the fastenings were to go and taken out and bored. In fastening the knees in you will find it practically impossible to hit the brads with a hammer as there is not room to swing one and the only way I could get the brad in was to enter it in the bored hole and then with a pair of tweezers squeeze the brad up into place in the beam.

There is still another knee to be fitted to the mast beams and that is what are known as "lodge knees." They lay on the shelf horizontally and clamp and the arm goes out against the deck beam. There is one of them to every main beam that crosses the ship. There also should be a hanging knee to every mast beam and to the main beams at each end of the hatchways, so the knees are pretty evenly spaced throughout the length of the ship to give it uniformity of strength.

The corner made by the deck and the side of the ship is a weak spot that must be securely stiffened by knees. So important was this considered by the old-time, wood-ship builders that the rules of those days called for one hanging knee and two horizontal, or lodge knees, at the ends of each deck beam. That is why in scanning the old plans we see such a multitude of knees shown. The weight of the deck cannon, then carried by all vessels, and the straining of the spars and sails on the deck frame of vessels, required that this strength be put in to counteract it.

But they did not have a deck beam at every frame as we have in this brig, their beams being spaced as much as four or five feet apart. But they did have, besides these main beams, many carlings and smaller beams. In the case of the ten-gun brig *Alert*, whose plans I have before me, only 21 deck beams are shown, but we must remember that these are only her main or heavy beams. Could we see the full lay-out of all her deck frames, it would tell us an entirely different story.

After the mast beams are in, the next to locate are the hatch beams, a heavy one to be located at each end of each hatchway. The main hatch in our brig comes so close to the mainmast that the foremost mast partner beam acts as the after beam of this hatch.

The fore and aft carlings, that form the hatch opening, are the thickness of the beam but wide enough so that there is room on it not only for the hatch coaming to set but also room for the ends of the deck planking to land and fasten to. In our case this means ⅜-inch wide. Halve the ends of these carlings into the beams as was done for the mast partners. Knee-off the ends of these hatch beams to the frames the same as the partner beams. The short beams at these hatches are to have their inboard ends dovetailed into the carlings. To fill in the wide span between the mast beams, lighter deck beams are fitted in, their ends being let into beveled notches cut in the knee at the side of the ship and into the knees at the partner plank. You will find that this variation in the size of beams adds considerable to the attractiveness of your model. I know it stimulated me to a greater desire to continue the work to see it grow towards completion, and it stimulated Teddy to stop in more often to see how she was coming on.

Be careful as you fit in beams to see that they line up to a level surface on top where the covering-board has to lay or you will come to grief later. If need be, insert small shims under the ends of your beams, although, of course, you want to make everything an absolutely perfect fit if you can. But it seems a shame to throw away an otherwise perfect beam just because it lacks ¹⁄₆₄ inch at the end, or perhaps the shelf was not 100 per cent perfect.

Under each main beam, in the middle of their length, there should be a stanchion to give it support, and this will be found a great source of strength to the hull as a whole. Make them about $\frac{3}{16}$-inch square, of black walnut. Bore a hole in each end of the stanchion and another in the keelson directly under the center of the beam, and put in dowels to hold them from shifting. Then plumb-up the stanchion and bore down through the deck beam and dowel it there. The crushing strains on a real ship's deck are sometimes very excessive. You cannot imagine how, in a gale of wind, the ship will roll, and when she happens to roll at the time when an unusually heavy sea crests up and tons of water, impelled by a gale of wind blowing at 60 miles an hour, come crashing against the flat of her deck laid over, just at that time, at an angle that catches the weight squarely on the deck. It is then the sailor's life depends on the strength of the hold stanchions as they prevent the decks from crushing in and sinking the ship. These stanchions, in a real ship, are kneed-off to both the keelson and deck beams, for when a ship is rolled over on her beam's ends, there is a great pressure exerted to squeeze the ship together and this tends to buckle up the deck beam so it pulls up from the stanchion. It is the function of these knees to prevent the beam and the stanchion from separating.

An interesting bit of detail can be worked in here, on merchant ship models, by cutting a staggered set of notches down the edges of the stanchions that face into the hatchways. The sailors climb up these notches like monkeys and wear a broad grin to see the portly port officials, when they have to go below for the purpose of an inspection, have a ladder put down the hatch before they dare venture below, and even then half of them do not know enough to face the ladder. Where not kneed, stanchions are strapped to the beams by iron straps with several bolts in each member.

When you have all the beams in and all the knees fastened, plane up a strip of pine the same thickness as the depth of the deck beam and ½-inch wide. Cut sections of this strip to fit to a jamb tightness between the ends of each beam end, laying on top of the clamp and shelf, and fasten it with a brad. These are not only a source of considerable stiffness to the hull, holding all the deck frame solid, but they answer another purpose as well. They give something to nail the waterways and the nibbing strake to, and form a ledge to pick up the ends of the deck plank between the beams. These blocks of pine, being all cut from a single piece, are all the same thickness and will line up, or should line up, with the top of the deck beams. They act as a gauge to see that all the beams are true and if they do not line up, they should be made to before you are done with them. Up in the bows, against the stem, fill up on top of the shelf with pine, "ekeing" as it is called, so it ends fair with the deck beams and the deck planking will have something to nail to there.

It is a rather long and unsupported span across the ship, for those beams that have no stanchions under them. In house carpentry this would be corrected by bridging, as the X-like, cross-bracing between the beams is called; but in shipbuilding we fit short sections of a smaller sized beam between each set of beams. These pieces are let into the main beams and jogged in for half their depth, which supports and stiffens the beam and gives a nailing surface for the deck planking. There is a set of these stiffeners on each side of the ship, run in a fore-and-aft line with the edge of the hatch coamings, extending from bow to stern. All this takes a lot of very fine cutting and fitting, but you can thank your lucky stars that you are not building a three-decker, for there the deck construction is twice as complicated and there are several decks to build instead of only one, as in this case.

If you do not have something to guide you, but just go ahead and fit in the deck beams at haphazards, you will find, when completed, that the deck line, fore and aft, is a series of hills and hollows. Avoid this by having a fairly stiff batten, say ⅜-inch square, and with small screw clamps, such as the five and ten cent stores sell, or used to sell, clamp this batten down the center line of your brig's deck and set the beams so they all align true with it.

In framing the deck, as in many other operations in shipbuilding, the most difficult thing is not merely to put the beams across, that is too obviously necessary, but it is to make all the little provisions for the fittings that are to come. Sometimes, if forgotten, it is impossible later to put in something that should have gone in when the deck was framed. That is where a proper plan to study over and see what is needed is of great help, especially to one none too familiar with the mode of procedure. For instance, where the pumps go down through the deck to the bilge, a filling-block of pine should be fitted between the beams. Where the bowsprit bitts fit in, a similar packing of pine should be provided. The carlings, if not made wider than the hatch coamings, will leave the deck unsupported and that is why wide deck beams are fitted at each end of each hatchway to leave some of the beam's surface clear of hatch coamings, to give room for the ends of the deck planking to fasten to.

Along the waterways, at the sides of the ship, we have made provision for the deck plank ends with the ½-inch wide chocks of pine fitted between the ends of the beams inside of the frames; but other ships may be constructed differently.

There is a variety of ways in which this part of the ship is constructed. The space between the beams affords ventilation and usually is left open, so the chocks are made much shallower and notched into the beams. Another way is to mark a line, indicating where the seam between the deck plank and the nibbing strake will come, and fit in a set of chocks along this line so there will be wood under the plankends when you come to caulk the deck seams and also something to fasten the nib ends of the deck planking to, so they will not be "springboards." Instead of chocks, a score can be cut out of the top of each beam and a long strip bent in, forming a locking strake for the same purpose.

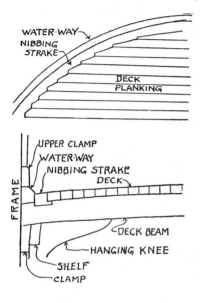

The "nib ends," referred to, are the ends of planks that, instead of being left tapered to a sharp point, as would be the case around the bow, are chopped off or "nibbed off" so their ends are squared off to about two inches, or so a narrow caulking iron could be used there. The strake of deck planking size, that is bent around just inside of the waterways, or covering-board, as some call it, is notched out or "nibbed," to receive the partially squared-off deck plank ends. The deck plank might be four inches wide, so from where its outer edge meets the nibbing strake, it is tapered to the two inch wide "nib" that starts where the inner (nearer amidships) edge crosses the nibbing strake. This gives the end of the deck plank a scarph-like cut and this shape is marked on and chiseled out of the nibbing strake. This process of nib-bing avoids thin shim ends, a fault never permitted in shipbuilding.

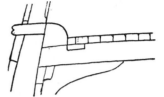

WATER WAYS ON 880 TON BARK JAMES-A-WRIGHT.

Waterways on vessels of war were very different from those on merchant vessels. Not, however, in the early merchantmen and even in those down to about 1820, when every deep-water man had to carry cannon for protec-tion against pirates or an enemy country's ships. The carrying of cannon was the

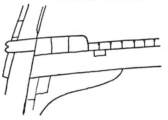

WATER WAYS ON 3 MAST SCHOONER J. PERCY - BARTRAM. 371 TONS.

cause of this difference in construction. The merchant ships I went to sea on, in the 1890's, had waterways that stuck up a foot above the decking and were two or three feet wide. You could not have operated a gun-carriage on such a deck. There the deck had to be level and the waterways were nothing but a chamfered-corner chock permitting the wheels of the gun car-riage to go clear to the bulwarks so that the muzzle of the gun would be out from the ship's side.

The bulwarks on men-of-war were sheathed up, in-side and out, with hard woods,—woods such as elm, picked out because they were tough enough to stop small bullets and not inclined to be shattered into dangerous flying splinters as destructive as cannon balls themselves to human beings crowded on the fighting deck of a ship. To match up flush with this inside sheathing in the waist, the waterways were made the same thickness, so that the bulwark and decking were flush surfaces meeting in the corner where the waterways, chamfered off to 45 degrees, formed a fillet in the corner.

After cutting down any unfair frames that may protrude on the inside of your model, fit in a fillet-like strip for a waterway, made out of a quarter-inch square strip of either black walnut, mahogany or teak. The latter makes, perhaps, the best looking ship if you can procure it and is what was largely used, especially on English ships, as that country imported much of it in the old East Indiamen that traded regularly to India. Americans used white oak, mostly, for all such purposes, as it was more easily obtained than either oak or elm.

I made the waterways out of mahogany. The after end, cut beveling so it ended against the transom, was clamped at intervals and even at the last moment before fastening it in, there were one or two timberheads that had to be shaved off a little so it eased the line of the waterways into a fairer curve. Boring between each timber from the outside, I fastened the waterways with small ⅜-inch bunghead brads.

The waterways bent in cold as far as the sixth frame from the bow, breast the foremast, and from here I sawed them out to shape, a piece on each side, to abreast the last (after) hawse timber and then a piece across the bow connecting the two. Butt joints will do here, as the deck and the waist cover all but the small chamfered face of the waterways, so only what looks like the nib end of a scarph will be seen when it is finished. Scarphs in waterways should be scarphed vertically, so the seam may be caulked like any deck seam, where, as in a merchant ship, the waterways are wide, heavy timbers.

On top of this waterway against the frames, an upper clamp strake is next to be bradded fast. It extends from the knightheads forward to the transom aft and is so thin it can be got out in one piece and bent in and sprung edgewise, a parallel strip of mahogany $\frac{1}{16}$-inch thick and $\frac{5}{16}$-inch wide, or just even with the port sills (see midship section). Forward, these are finished off by a thick piece of mahogany $2\frac{1}{2}$-inches long and as deep as is necessary to fill in under the knee or breast hook that unites the inner rail stringer at the stem, down to the waterways. Shape this so it fits in against the stem, knightheads and hawse timbers, rabbeting it out to lap over the ends of the inner rail stringer above and the upper deck clamp below. Then cut it all down to about $\frac{1}{8}$-inch thickness so it finishes off flush with the inner edge of the waterways. Round off the after edges of the ends. This reenforcement is appropriate as the hawse holes come through it. But this is a little premature as we must first size down the heads of our timbers and frame the gun ports.

We are now confronted with the problem of regulating the top-timbers and framing the portholes. As the size of the porthole depends on the size of the cannon we must first decide on the armament our little brig is to carry and history tells us the *Lexington* carried four pounders. The diameter of a four-pound shot was 3.053 inches, and the rule for determining the size of gun ports, etc., was as follows: gun ports are spaced apart, center to center, 25 times the diameter of the shot. The gun port's length, fore and aft, should be 6½ diameters; the height, six diameters; and the sill or lower edge of the port should be 3½ diameters above the deck. By this rule our portholes should be 6.36 feet apart at a minimum; their length, fore and aft, 19.8 inches; their height, 15.28 inches; and the sill, 10.69 inches above the deck.

In order to avoid trouble later in laying out the location of these gun ports, reference must be made to the sail plan or rigging plan, to so space the ports as to least interfere with the shrouds and the ship's rigging. This is a fairly simple matter in the case of our little brig, but a serious one when you come to a two- or a three-decker. Here, sometimes, straddle chain plates have to be resorted to, and channels, as the platforms that hold the shrouds out and away from the ship's side, are called, have to be stopped, after the lower shrouds are accommodated. Separate platforms, channels, or as they were termed in the old days, "stools," were then provided, farther aft for the backstays and raised up above the line of the main channel as was often the case, especially at the mizzenmast, in order to clear the gun muzzles. In our brig, this has been laid out so that while the space has been increased between the forward or bridle port as it is termed, and the second port, to provide room for the fore-lower shrouds, none of her ports are spaced closer than the minimum of 6.36 feet which experience has proved was as close as the four-pound guns could be set and give the guns' crew room to work without interference. Her backstays all come down to the same channel as the main rigging, as her portholes are so small they come below the channels.

The next step is to figure out which top-timbers will make the two sides of each port. By measuring from our plan these prove to be the following, viz.: the first port between frameheads Nos. 5 and 6; the second between Nos. 10 and 11; the third between Nos. 13 and 14; the fourth between Nos. 16 and 17; the fifth between Nos. 19 and 20; the sixth between Nos. 22 and 23; the seventh between Nos. 27 and 28; and the eighth and aftermost between frames Nos. 30 and 31, as the frames are numbered on our plan and which coincide with those of the model which is being built as this story progresses.

The width of the gun ports called for by the shot-diameter rule, is about two inches wider than the space between our timberheads which will just permit us to shave them down to a neat finish. If the ports had been wider it would have necessitated our sawing off a timber and setting in an auxiliary piece in the space between the two frames. Or we could have so laid out our futtocks that they might have spanned the port by letting the reverse timberhead extend up to the rail height, so that instead of a 16-inch opening, we would have had a 24-inch space between timber-tops.

It is the complexity of all these port openings, in the frame of a three-decker, that makes them so difficult to build, and unless one has a plan whereon all this has been carefully figured out and delineated, I would not advise anyone to attempt such a structure until they have experienced the troubles that beset one in constructing a single-decked vessel.

Having located where the portholes are to go we must fair up the outside at the deck edge and all the top-timbers to the rail height. You can do this best with a large file about 15 to 18 inches long, finishing off with fine sandpaper. In order to be able to see when these top-timbers are fair it is necessary to cut them all down to the proper sheer heights. Mark the rail heights at intervals of about every fourth frame, taking your measurement from the sheer plan, and then bend a small batten to these marks. When you have a sweet, fair curve, with no kinks in it to offend the eye, mark

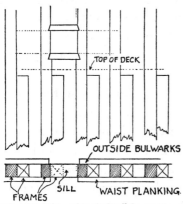

TOP OF DECK

OUTSIDE BULWARKS

FRAMES   SILL   WAIST PLANKING.
HOW PORTS ARE FORMED AND
PORT SILLS FITTED IN PLACE.

each timber and then saw it off to this mark, parallel with the crown of the deck beam, athwartships. You will need this slight outward tilt to mate in with the rail across the transom at the stern.

With the timberheads so trimmed off and faired up on the outside, you now have a more delicate task and need a very sharp knife or small chisel (both, perhaps, as the grain of the wood may have to be cut downward in one place and upward in the next) to size-down all the timberheads to a uniform thickness. As ours is a war craft and her bulwarks are to be ceiled up inside, this is all that is necessary, but were she a merchant vessel, with these timbers all exposed below the pinrail, they would have to be slightly tapered in their siding and the inner edges chamfered off as well, and sandpaper finished for painting.

When you have the timberheads sized up to equal thickness, the gun ports can be framed by cutting notches and fitting in the upper and lower port sills. Make these out of black walnut or whatever wood you have used in the framing of your ship. Plane down a strip ⅛ inch in thickness and a little wider than your timberheads so you can have a little wood to file off and make a perfectly flush job.

Be careful to get these port sills accurately in line with the sweep of the deck edge, both top and bottom sills, or they will hurt the vessel's appearance to the eye. Remember that in ship work it is the little details that make or spoil a good model. Have the sills horizontal in the athwartships direction. The sills are flush with the inside ceilings or waist strakes and the out-side planking is set flush and then has a small recess cut around the two sides and bottom of the porthole to form a rabbet to receive the correspondingly rabbeted

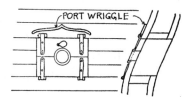

PORT WRIGGLE OVER PORT.

edge of the port lid, to make it at least partially water tight. The top edge is left a square-edged drip. On the two- and three-deckers and even on frigates, where the sides tumbled home, generally there were "port wriggles,"—little fancy mouldings above each gun port, arched to carry the water off on either side of the porthole.

But that is getting ahead of the work we have in hand. As before we should finish the inside of our bulwarks first and put the outside strakes on afterwards. In putting in the waterways around the sweep of the bow, if you cannot get it in after softening it with hot steam, without breaking it, jig saw it out of a wide piece as you did the shelf. Where it joins the side pieces cut a scarph joint, although a butt will not be so bad at this particular place, as the clamp to be fitted on top of it and the nibbing strake or deck against it will hide so much of it that the kind of joint here will be hidden from view. Do not let fastenings show but with a fine nail-punch drive them in so that tiny bits of beeswax can be squeezed in to cover them. Of course this should be done with wooden plugs fitted so snug into holes counterbored for them that they would hardly be seen in the real ship; but we can hardly expect to be so microscopic in our work as to fit in wood plugs, so we must do the next best thing which is to use plastic wood. If you can't get plastic wood, then collect a clean pile of sawdust (sandpaper dust) and mix it into a thick paste, with glue, and then fill the holes with it. This will match up in color with the wood and is particularly recommended in places where the woodwork is to be left natural.

It will be a source of much satisfaction if you take a few moments' time to make up a dummy or quaker gun out of pine and a rough gun carriage made so that the gun is the right height above the deck. Don't put on any axles or wheels. Leave the block square on the bottom and try this gun in your gun ports to avoid any future trouble and be sure it is workable, and can be elevated and depressed and is not hard down on the port sills. Make the center of your gun 18 inches above the deck. The cannon should be six feet long, the trunnion $2\frac{3}{4}$ feet from the cascable to the center of the trunnion or $3\frac{1}{4}$ feet from the muzzle. The cannon are ten inches in diameter at the cascable and six inches at the muzzle. These measurements are not the finished sizes for your cannon but only for making rough dummy guns to try in your portholes.

The next move is to securely tie up the heads of the top-timbers, by fastening a strake ten inches wide, of parallel width from bow to stem, along the timbers to the exact sheer line as given in the plan. Put an oak, or teak, or mahogany stringer strake inside and an oak strake outside and brad them to the timberheads all of which must be reduced to the same size so these strakes will lay fair.

Do not carry the timberhead up too heavy or it will make the top rail to cover them so wide as to look clumsy. The classification society's rules limit us, however, to a minimum of $5\frac{1}{2}$ inches square for a craft of this size. With a 3-inch stringer strake inside and a 3-inch strake outside, this gives us $11\frac{1}{2}$ inches, and the rail, to show moulded edges, will have to be about 14 inches wide. You will find it easy to put in the inner rail stringer, if you use oak. It can be bent in cold it is so thin. Cut a piece of wood as a gauge and slide it on a deck beam until it hits the timberheads and stringer; then bring the stringer just flush with it and screw-clamp it fast. Do this at intervals all along inside the bulwark and your stringers will run parallel with the deck at the side. Bore for every hole. First near the upper edge, then on the next frame, near the lower one alternately and toe the fastenings in, staggered so the upper ones go diagonally a little forward and the lower ones a little aft. They hold better than if driven in parallel. The brad points will come through but let them; so long as you have bored clear through, the frame will not split. You can snip their points off and then later with a large file dress them and the wood down to an even thickness.

This stringer fastens to the inside of the knuckle timber and is sawed off flush with the after side of it. Forward fit in a hook or knee that can be nailed to the inside of the stem and lap back along on the stringer to the second hawse timber, to which it and others can be bradded. This makes a neat and strong finish and ties both sides together. I used a piece of white ash for this knee as its color matched well with the oak and I happened to have some seasoned aeroplane stock; but oak or any hard wood will answer. Make it as wide as the stringer and round the ends and finish nicely for, although the bowsprit hides most of it, the two arms will show in the completed ship. This stringer will stiffen all the top-timbers. If you have a fine-tooth saw you can saw along with the stringer as a guide and cut off all the tops of the timbers and the frameheads, and smooth them off with a file or sandpaper. Leave the knightheads, however, to be finished off later.

At this point I gave the whole frame another coat of linseed oil, Theodore having given the frame a good coat when he stopped work on it six years ago, but this had dried so that where it was filed it showed very much lighter in color. This coating of oil darkened it to an even color. I then took it to a photographer to get some good pictures to show how she had been built up to this time, and I also measured and checked off the frames and beams and made a construction plan. I had made and put on the three hatch coamings because sometimes, as when the frame was wet with oil, I could not work on it, and so worked on other details, making the bowsprit, bitts, rudder, etc.

It is not out of order for us now to consider the hatch coamings because they must go on before any decking can be done as they bolt right onto the deck frame. To insure uniformity in size, plane up a strip of black walnut, ⅜ by 9, scant ¼ inch. It takes nine inches for the fore hatch, ten inches for the main and eight inches for the mizzen hatch, so get out about 30 inches of this sized stock; then mark out on these pieces the exact size of each hatch opening and before you halve the corners together cut a rabbet in the top inner edges to receive the hatch covers, the same thickness as the deck planking. I made it four inches. This can be sawed out of the two side pieces, but the "headers," at the ends, will have to be chiseled out so as to leave a corner piece standing to meet the sides, for the headers form the top half when you match the coamers together. Bore and brad each corner, keeping the hatch a true, square corner. Then round the underside of the headers to fit the crown of the deck beam. Lay a piece of sandpaper on the beam and rub the hatch across it to finish to an accurate fit, and then brad the hatch to the deck frame, using two brads in each piece, near each corner, and "stagger" or slant the brads a little. Here you will note that by using a wide deck beam at each hatch opening, you will have about one-third of the beam left exposed to form a landing for the ends of the deck planking.

The bowsprit bitts also require attention at this point as their lower ends have to be fastened. To make them, take a piece of black walnut $\frac{5}{16}$ by $\frac{3}{16}$ of an inch (equivalent to 10 inches by 6 inches in the real ship) and $4\frac{5}{16}$ inches (11 feet, 6 inches) long. Leave them full size at the top for $1\frac{1}{2}$ inches (4 feet) and then bevel down to about $\frac{3}{16}$-inch (6 inches) square at the lower ends. Mark your center line accurately on the deck beam, aft of which they fit (aft of the third beam, in our case) and cut out holes to let the bitts go through the pine filler between the beams and fit their lower ends so they match fair against the limber strakes in the hold of the ship. Then bore up into each bitt leg and insert a dowel. Dip these ends in white paint and while it is fresh put the bitts back into place and push them down until the paint gives you a spot so you can see just where to bore a couple of holes to receive the dowels in the bitts, but do not fasten the bitts yet as the deck has to be put on first.

Between the bitts, which are set ½ inch (16 inches) apart, there should be a "bolster piece" ⁵⁄₁₆ by ³⁄₁₆ of an inch (9 inches by 6 inches) set horizontally so its top is ⅜ inch (12 inches) below the top of the bitts, notched partly out of the bolster and partly out of the after side of the bitt posts so the bolster projects aft of the bitts ⅛ inch (4 inches). Bore and brad the bolster fast. The bolster is 1½ inches (4 feet) long, the arms projecting ⁵⁄₁₆ inch (10 inches in scale) on each side. To receive the heel of the bowsprit, fit snug a solid block of ¼-inch pine, or hard wood, if you wish, between the bitts snug under the bolster and brad it in with a brad near the top and bottom on each side, leaving the middle clear to chisel a mortise for the tenon that is to be cut on the inboard end of your bowsprit and fit into this mortise. If you do all this before you fit the bitts through the deck, and then fit the bitts as a unit, you will find it easier to make a snug fit.

Now to finish the inside of the bulwarks. There is about nine inches from the waterways to the port sills. So a clamp strake worked in here from bow to stern is our next job. This is 3-inch stuff which is about ³⁄₃₂ of an inch in actual size and as it is to be painted it can be made of pine or oak. To find the shape around the bow, bend in a piece of thin cardboard or stiff paper and scribe the shape up from the waterways and cut this out and use as a pattern to shape the wood. With this clamp in, the intervening space can be filled in in short lengths between the ports. Around the bow bend one piece, and the clamp will look better if done the same way. The waist will end at the forward port, the bow-chase port, between the first and second frameheads. The headrails will just permit a gun being fired from this port and in fact should be laid out so it can be done without shooting away part of the ship. Such a gun cannot be depressed for close range work, but that is not the function of a bow chase. It is to try to cripple a fleeing vessel by shooting away some spar or raking her fore and aft to make her change her course.

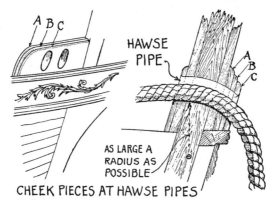

CHEEK PIECES AT HAWSE PIPES

Up in the bows, away up in the very eyes of her, the jumble of frames can all be neatly covered with a heavy hawse piece, carved, hollow and round, out of pine. This extends to the side of the bow-port and can be made in one piece or seamed at the center line. That is how we made it, with a vertical center piece for each side to butt against, the reenforcement previously referred to. This is not merely ornamental but serves a most useful purpose. Where the hawsers go through the bows the underside of the holes are made as large an arc of a circle as the construction will permit so the hawsers will bend easier and not be cramped over a corner which would not only tend to wear out the heavy rope, by bending the fibers too sharply, causing them to rupture, but the men at the capstan bars would quickly feel the difference when they tried to heave in the anchor. The larger the radius, or sheave, as it were, the easier the hawser will come in.

It is for the purpose of increasing this radius that we see the three layers of padding rounded off on the outside, which in old plans may look like mere ornamental work.

The aim is to tie up the timberheads before we proceed with the hull, for we cannot very well handle the craft to clean her up for the outside planking without carrying something away if we leave the frameheads unfinished. So after we have the inside rail stringer in we should put on the outer stringer. These two steady the caprail which lands on top of them. Level the tops of the two across or give a slight tilt downward on the outer edge. I finally levelled mine across all the way, from the bows back to within a short distance of the stern, from about the last gun port, and then let the outer stringer run a little lower than the inner one, which slightly canted the rail so it would mate in with the crown of the rail across the stern, the taffrail as it is termed.

On a model, where it can be done so easily, I took a thin piece of oak, about 3-inches wide, that I was intending to cut my outer rail stringer out of, and I held it against the side of the model and scribed out the sheer line with a lead pencil, following the curve made by the inner stringer. This is not "ship-building," I know, but it is "model-building," and when we come to the subject of planking we will explain in full just how planks, stringers, clamps, etc., are laid out and "spiled," to find their actual shape on the changing bevels of the ship's frame, from the tumble home amidships, to the flam or flare of the bow.

This stringer, after the upper edge was decided, I sawed out a little wider than the distance from the underside of the rail (the shape just scribed out with a pencil), and the top of the gun ports. Just enough wood was left standing so I could make a fair curve of the *lower edge*. Then this was clamped in place on the model, the lower edge being the edge to fair up. Never mind the top edge; that can be run off with a file and faired up after it is fastened on in place.

Try the end forward and fit it accurately into the rabbet, which, if it is not yet cut or cut deep enough, must now be cleaned out to receive the end of the rail stringer. The sheer strake, the top plank of the regular side planking, the top wale strake, should, in a real ship, be the first plank to go on, but remember we are building a model. When it is fitted, clamp it in place and bore and fasten with two small brads, staggered in each framehead, or, if you find that too much iron for the small framehead (as we cannot get fastenings small enough to follow every detail perfectly) put one brad in each framehead or top-timber, as we called it when framing. Stagger them, putting one near the top of the stringer and at the next frame one near the bottom of it, then the next near the top, and so on, the whole length. Put one fastening, at least, in every frame. We probably could not get her classed at Lloyds or the American Bureau of Shipping, if their inspectors got onto this fact, yet they might consider the excess in size of fastening used as compensation for lack of number of fastenings and so pass her. Be very careful when you put on the stringer on the other side, to see that they match up in perfect alignment at the bow, and watch the hump or shoulder as you bend it around the bluff of the bow and get both sides level across. Saw the after ends off flush with the rake of the transom. These two, the inner and outer rail stringers line up on their lower edges with the top of the gun ports.

With a long file dress off the top edges of both outer and inner stringers and any intervening timberheads

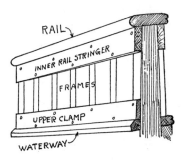

that may show up above them, as the model will now be stiff enough to stand such filing.

If this were a real ship we should leave each timberhead about 1½ inches higher than the stringers, so cut these down to a tenon about 4 to 6 inches square and then chisel corresponding mortices out of the underside of the caprail. If you want to do this, don't let me stop you from doing it, but it is a nice job both to lay it out and to cut it. I put my rail on "flat-footed."

It is some satisfaction to see the rail going on. The time, in hour's work, on my model, at this time, ready for her rails, was 240 hours. But the finished appearance a model takes on when the timberheads are no longer to be seen, makes one feel he is making progress.

A wide piece of ⅛-inch mahogany laid on the clamps and timberheads, permitted the shape of the caprail to be scribed out, and after shaping and fairing up the outer edge, the width of the rail, 15 inches, was scaled off and the piece cut out parallel with the shaped edge. Finish the inner edge so it has, as nearly as possible, an even amount of overhang all along its length and round the corners off; then fair the outer edge the same way. I find the best way is to hold it under a bright light and note the shadows, that and by feeling, i.e., by running your fingers along and gripping the edges of the rail, will tell you where it overhangs more or less. But while you want this even, remember also that you want a rail the same width all along from bow to stern. It may be that the stringers are not exactly fair. If so, drive in shim wedges, as wide as the frames, and force the stringer out until it makes a true, fair line. If you are a 100% perfect workman you will need no shims, but every ship that went to sea, you can gamble, had some shims.

SCRAPER TO MOULD EDGES of RAIL.

Why, even the ceiling in the hold was caulked with the shim end of shingles driven in as wedges. I admit I resorted to a few shims and you will do the same if you want a fair-lined ship. In building this model as I write I have brought to my attention many little points of construction that might have been overlooked if I had trusted to a memory of bye-gone days. Necessarily I have worked faster on this model than I would have done if it were purely a hobby, where one doesn't want to hurry.

When you have the outer edges fair, mould them into a double-round, a molding almost universal in American ships and neat, in that it made the otherwise heavy-looking edge, light and graceful. Take a piece of brass, almost any metal will do, and file out the shape for your rail's edge, and with this scrape the edge, lightly at first, until you mould it to the required shape.

Cut hook-scarphs when you cut out the two pieces

that go around the bluff of the bow and finish out the rail on each side up to the knightheads. Across the stern, a piece of rail, the taffrail, was fitted beveling against the transom and landing on top of the knuckle frames that were trimmed off fair to receive it. Mitre-joint

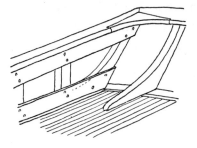

the corners with the rail and fit in a small knee in each corner. Instead of cutting an arched or crowned taffrail, I finally fitted mine in level across as the rails were so nearly level it made a neater fin-

ish and the arch of the stern was carried out by the top of the transom which crowned up in the middle ¼ inch above the taffrail, coming down to nothing, or flush, at the corners, and finished off with a caprail to match the main rail, being let down at the corners until the moulded edges met in a perfect joint.

The lower transom may be planked across horizon-tally in small planks, if you wish, or in one wide piece with seams scratched in. The latter is the easier on

account of the rudderport that cuts several of the low-er strakes in two. To fas-ten these ends, the diagonal pieces that butted against the sternpost and formed the rudderport, should be

deep enough to extend to the outside of the planking and have a rabbet cut in them to receive the transom planking so they may be caulked and made water-tight. Let the ends of the transom extend past the side far enough to cover the ends of the side planking. Leave too much, rather than too little, as it can easily be trimmed off after the planking is on.

We are now ready to put on the first strake of planking, called the top strake or sheer strake, as it outlines the sheer of the ship. A "strake" is merely the shipbuilder's term for "plank." The planking-up of our little single-decked ship is a simple matter compared to that of one of the old-time ships, the three-deckers with their outside planking divided into many belts of varying thickness between the many heavy belts of wale strakes.

William Sutherland, shipbuilder and mariner, in 1775 published a most interesting little book called the *Shipbuilder's Assistant*. In this we can get a good idea of the wale strakes of a 500-ton ship of his day which had a lower wale 1 foot 2 inches wide by 8½ inches thick. The upper wale was 11½ inches by 8 inches; the lower chain wale, 8⁷⁄₁₀ inches by 4⁷⁄₁₀ inches; and the upper chain wale, 8⁴⁄₁₀ inches by 4³⁄₁₀ inches. The wale strakes on ships of the early 1800's were a belt of thick plank at the widest part of the ship, the planks above and below gradually diminishing to the thin bottom plank and to the rail. The channel wales, abreast of the main deck, were lighter than the main wales that came just abreast the lower deck beam ends about at the water line. The channels butted against the sheer strakes abreast the upper deck beams and these strakes were a little thicker than the adjoining plank. When the clipper ships were in their prime, the classification societies formulated rules to regulate their construction. In their case there was a certain depth of these thick planks to insure vertical strength. The American Bureau of Shipping says in Section 28, "The vertical extent of the wales should equal one-third of the vessel's depth of hold. For vessels whose length is eight and more depths, the width of the wales must be two-fifths of the depth of hold."

The Lloyd's rules, in 1870, read as follows: "The breadth of the wales in every case is to be regulated as under, viz.: — When the extreme length of the ship, measured from the fore part of the stem to the after part of the sternpost on the range of the upper deck, is six times her depth of hold (and under), the wales are to be in breadth 3 inches, to every foot of the depth of hold. When the extreme length of the ship is eight times her depth of hold the wales are to be in breadth 3½ inches to every foot of the depth of hold. When the extreme length of the ship is ten times her depth of hold (and above) the wales are to be in breadth 4 inches to every foot of the depth of hold."

There were strict rules laid down governing all the vitals of a ship. Certain woods were allowed just so many years for each part of the ship's structure — for the keel, live oak, teak, locust and greenheart were given 18 years, while oak, white oak and the oaks of Southern Europe were given 12 years; red oak, 9 years; yellow pine, 8 years, etc., etc. Hackmatack is only given an allowance of life of 7 years as a keel, but when used for knees its length of life increased to 12 years. Tables of these societies show what each kind of wood may be used for and the number of years that experience has found it safe to leave them there. There was no guesswork about shipbuilding. The size of each timber, likewise, is given for ships of various tonnages, and compliance with these rules was demanded if the ship wished to be classified and get the lowest rates of insurance.

What some amateur shipbuilders cannot seem to

grasp, is the fact that there is as much difference between the structure of a small 700-ton ship and a 2500-
ton ship, as there is between the building of a cottage
and a skyscraper. One such, who never sailed on a ship
in his life or saw one built, claims that because the
wales of a 2000-ton ship in a newspaper description he
read, were not as I described them for the 700-ton *Sea
Witch*, my description of the latter's wales was all
wrong.

Our first consideration is to find out what size our
wales for a craft the size we are building should be.
By Lloyd's rule the thickness is 4 inches and a total
breadth of 36 inches; while by the American Bureau
of Shipping, 3½ inches in thickness is given, but the
total breadth compensates by making it 42 inches. The
Raven, 18-gun British brig-of-war, built in 1804 (a
copy of whose specifications is given in the appendix)
shows this 100 foot by 30 foot by 12 foot 9 inches. The
brig had two 4½-inch strakes of wales 12 inches wide,
each of them, then one strake of 3½-inch oak, and a
fourth (the diminishing strake as it is termed) that
tapered from 3½-inches thick at its upper edge to 3-
inches on its lower edge where it matched the rest of
her side and bottom planking. Her sheer strake was
3-inch fir. Sea and shipbuilding phrases are most am-
biguous for the novice, so remember that the wales are
strakes of heavy planking and that there are gunwales,
middle wales, main wales, and channel wales.

We will use in the *Lexington*, she being a war-vessel,
the 4-inch thickness of wales, and use four strakes,
each 10-inches wide amidships. An unwritten rule in
planking is the 5-4-3 rule, which means the proportions the width of each plank should endeavor to assume to make a neat looking ship when the topsides

are planked up, viz. — five amidships, four forward, and three aft. So chalk off 40 inches down on the midship frame where the bottom of the wales will come with four 10-inch strakes. Forward, the depth should be ⅘ of this and aft, ⅗ of it. So forward chalk off a mark 32 inches down, and aft, 24 inches below where the top edge of the upper wales is to come.

How are we to find the shape of this top edge so a plank will lie true along with the edge of the deck level? In a real ship, of course, this could not be made all in one length of plank, but in our little brig it might be made in two pieces butted together amidships. I made mine all in one piece, however, on the model. You can take a piece of stiff cardboard, a little longer than the model and about an inch wide. A little width is preferable to a narrow batten, so it will not spring edgewise but act as the plank will when you put it on. Clamp this cardboard strip or, better yet, a thin wide (1¼ to 1½ inch) shim of wood, as I did, happening to have such a shim cut off a pine board, up against the side of the model so it comes just under the deck edge amidships. Then bend the ends around naturally with no forcing up or down, or buckling of the edges. Then with a pair of compasses or dividers, mark or prick off a row of dots parallel, a given distance to which the dividers are set equal to the greatest space down from the deck edge, the line where you want the top edge of the plank to come.

This cardboard or strip is called a "spiling staff." On it, where you prick off these distances, rule a straight line vertically at each spot and set the distance off on this line and then, when you mark back these spots on the plank itself, which you wish to shape, apply the measurement back along these same marks. The same result can be accomplished in various other ways, but this way has proved by experience to be the most practical. For instance, instead of pricking off a certain distance that the divider or compass points were set apart at each interval along the "spiling staff," you could use a staff where the edge was planed up to a perfectly true straight edge and then mark at intervals the measurements in inches from it to the edge of the waterways, or line representing them on the outside of the frames, where the top edge of the top strake was to come.

The disadvantages of such a method is that the twist given to the "spiling staff," to make it lay flat against the frames, in going around some ship's bows where there is a heavy flare, would throw the straight edge down so far in other places, farther aft on the hull, as to make the set-off measurements run into feet and inches. Whereas, by taking a drawknife and roughly shaping the "spiling staff" so it approaches nearer to the shape of the finished plank, the interval of set-off can be measured in inches. It was to avoid error in measuring and remeasuring so many distances that ship carpenters set their compasses to a distance equal to the greatest interval or set-off, and pricked this same distance all along on the staff, a parallel distance below the desired line. Experience is the best teacher.

You will find it pays to use oak for these wale strakes as it may be bent around with little steaming or even cold, without breaking, if you thin the ⅛-inch thickness down, just a little around the bluff of the bows.

Take the "spiling staff" off the model when you have a sufficient number of spots pricked off, about every other frame is enough, and lay the staff out flat on the ⅛-inch oak you intend to use for the plank.

Hold it so it cannot shift and prick back a row of spots that will give you the development of the curve you want to shape the plank's upper edge to. Take away the "spile staff" when the spots are all transferred to the plank and with a batten bend a fair curve connecting all these spots and mark the shape. Then saw it out and plane and file it up true to the eye. Do not try to shape the lower edge exactly in attempting to get out your first plank, for you may find you have to dress off your upper edge of the plank when you try it in place on the model, — cut it a little full. In lining out the lower edge remember the 5-4-3 rule. Measure the width amidships 10 inches; $\frac{4}{5}$ of this for the bow end or 8 inches in width, and at the stern end, $\frac{3}{5}$ or 6 inches. Bend a batten in a fair line in lining out the shape of the lower edge of your plank so the planks' widths show a gradual diminishing toward each end, and shape it to a line so drawn.

Shape and fit the forward end into the rabbet which should be cut out to receive it and bore and fasten the plank on with $\frac{3}{8}$ inch No. 20 bung-headed brads that just drive snug into a hole bored with a No. 75 drill. Put one brad into the long framehead and one into the short head, cutting the plank off aft so it butts against the projecting lower transom. Shape the second wale strake by the same method, only this time you prick down and reproduce the shape of the lower edge of the wale strake you have just put on. Repeat this process until you have all four strakes of wales in place.

Instead of a small ship if our craft had happened to have been a frigate or larger ship, with a heavy tumble home to her topsides, our wales might not have come at the deck edge but would then have been down to form a strengthening belt at her widest point which, in such designs, was down about at the waterline. This served a double purpose for if an enemy could shoot a hole through a ship's planking at or near the waterline, she was hitting a vulnerable spot and one liable to sink a ship. So while the bottom plank might be 5 inches thick on a hundred-gun ship, at her main wales, at the waterline she would have planking a foot or so in thickness. Some of the deep, high-sided, big clippers belted their wale strakes down where they would give the hull the greatest support. The location of the wales depended entirely on the design of the ship.

This, four strakes, is all the top planking I put on my model, leaving the frames exposed around the turn of the bilge; but starting at the keel, now that the topsides are securely tied together and nothing left sticking up to be broken, when the model is taken off the stocks on which she had been ever since her keel was laid, the bottom can be gone over with a long file and faired up. Down along the rabbet the file cannot be used but cutting tools have to be employed. A sharp knife blade, thin enough to bend, I found the most useful. I have one of those chuck-handles that has three differently shaped thin blades. The rounded back of the file also came in handy to clean up the tuck of the stern where the three transom frames made a corner with the sternpost that was hard to work in. By trying with a small batten these and the last cant frame were dressed down until it bent in fair and landed true on the beveled bottom edge of the main transom up against the cross seam batten.

With the bottom frames filed off fair and the rabbet cut to receive the planking, the garboard strake next claims attention. But before we do that there is a most important detail, if it were a real ship, and that is the cutting of limber holes across the heels of all the frames, away down near the keel, so the bilge water will not lay in pools at each frame and become foul smelling from stagnation, but flow, as down a gutter, to where the pumps can suck it up and discharge it out on deck where it will run overboard out through the scuppers. The size called for by the American Bureau of Shipping, was 2½ inches wide by 1½ inches deep, cut on each side of the keel and not to be over a plank seam. At each end, forward between frames 6 and 7, and aft between frames 32 and 33, which is as far as the limber chains can run, fit a block with rounded off edge for the chain to reeve over as it leads up to where it can be left handy to get at in case the limbers get stopped up. By pulling this limber chain back and forth, the holes may be cleared of chips or dirt that might lodge under the frames. This is very important in the real ship but it will be so hidden in the model that it will not generally be noticed if left out. The limber strake in the bottom of the hold, alongside the keelson, is so called because it is directly over the limbers and it is by removing them that access is had to the limbers to clear out dirt or rubbish.

You cannot file off a real ship's frame as we can a model. The procedure there is different. Each plank is lined off. A chalk line stretched along the face of the frames shows up any high ones and these are dubbed off with an adze until the line sights true so the plank will bear evenly on the face of each frame. Each plank is so provided for before it is put on. This is what is meant when we hear the expression of "lining out her planking."

The shape of the garboard is found by the use of a "spiling staff," the same as was done for the top strake.

Roughly shape the forward end of the staff to fit the up curve the rabbet takes and hold the staff against the frames near the rabbet. Then with dividers set far enough apart to span the greatest space between the rabbet and "spiling staff," prick off a series of spots all along on the staff so you can prick that same distance back at each spot when you take the "spiling staff" off the boat and lay it out flat on a plank from which you intend to shape the garboard strake, and so reproduce a line the exact shape of the rabbet. In real work you also take off the bevel to fit the edge of the garboard accurately into the notch the rabbet is cut to on the ship, but on the $\frac{1}{8}$-inch thick model plank you can best bevel the edge by eye, but make a snug fit of it, just the same, even if it is not going to be caulked.

With the shape of the lower edge established the top edge is to be determined, and here you will note that in order to have the planking throughout the side of the ship, wider in the middle and narrower at each end, like the staves that form a barrel, it will be necessary to close up the space to be planked at the ends. With this in view the garboard should be made as wide as convenient, at the after end, to gain all you can. At the same time it must not be too extreme. In the case of our little brig, for illustration, while the garboard is 15 inches wide amidships, we can make the ends about 24 inches wide.

Then put on the first broad strake, 15 inches wide in the middle and 18 inches at the bow end, that is, frame number 9 forward, and aft, at frame number 36, make it 24 inches. Then work on a second broad strake of the same dimensions and we will have gained enough in height at the ends so the space at each end is narrower than at the middle.

Another way of doing this is to work in a stealer — a wedge-shaped piece that nibs about 2 inches into the top edge of the first broad strake and ends aft with a width of about 18 inches. By doing this the broad strakes need not be made quite so wide aft, and it is a good way to raise the planking aft. If you do it this way, shape the top edge of the first broad strake so it starts to sweep up fair with the top edge of the stealer some distance forward of where it nibs in. Shipbuilders took great pride in the fairness of the curves the planking lines made, fore and aft, and abhorred any sudden hump or angle which was termed an "anchor stock," that being the shape the under edge of an anchor stock is cut. Very large ships often have two or three stealers in their after planking.

The subject of planking is very great due to the size of the ship and the shape of side; the various thicknesses used, as called for by the classification societies for merchant ships, and as necessary in the case of the men-of-war, and for the conservation of timber. It may seem to a novice a contradiction when I say that the wales and diminishing plank on large men-of-war were worked into plank that conserved the timber as much as possible by using the tapered width which the tree naturally gave and which was not cut down to a parallel width of plank but was widest at a quarter of its length from one end. This was termed the "top and butt" method and was more popular than the "anchor-stock" method where the plank was widest in the middle and tapered each way to the end. One edge of these planks was straight, so when the tapered edges were matched together it made every

other seam line a straight one, with zigzag one
between.

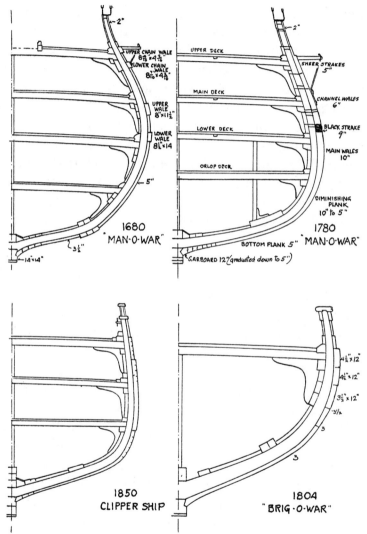

When I say a shipbuilder abhors an "anchor stock,"
I mean in the sense of its producing an unsightly un-
fairness in a line that catches the eye. As to the vari-

ous thicknesses of planking take, for example, the side of a line-of-battleship, a three-decker, where we have beginning at the top, just under the rail, the sheer strakes, channel wales, middle wales, black strake, main wale, diminishing plank, plank of the bottom, broad strakes, and garboards. The sheer strakes were those between the plank sheer and main deck ports. Between these and the ports of the middle deck, were the channel wales as they received the fastenings of the chain plates and preventer bolts to the channels. The middle wales were between the ports of the middle and lower decks. The planking between ports was termed short stuff. Below the lower deck ports came the black strake and then the main wales with the diminishing strakes below the wales tapering the heavy strakes down gradually to the thickness of the thin bottom planking. The few strakes next to the garboards were the broad strakes and then came the garboards, several of them in a large ship increasing in thickness to a heavy main garboard that rabbeted or notched into the side of the keel. Such was the plank on an eighteenth-century ship. On ships a century earlier the wale strakes were made more distinct from the surrounding plank as before described.

But let us get back to our little brig model. We have her wales on and below the garboard, first and second broad strakes and can leave her so unless you wish to put on one more plank to hide, a little more, the heels of the end frames, or you may wish to plank her up completely. I left mine open to show the frames as they define the shape of the hull better. However, we will proceed to plank her up completely as by so doing you will become acquainted with the use of what is termed the planking scale.

On a large clipper ship the side was "belted off" or divided into sections. Lines indicating the run of the planking at the top of the wales, the lower edge of the wales and about at the turn of the bilge, were laid off on the mould loft plan of the ship and then run on the ship's frame by bending battens along to these heights so they made fair-curved sweeps, fore and aft, and the line scribed-in across the face of the timbers. By doing this three gangs of plankers were able to carry on the work simultaneously, each planking up a certain belt of planking. On our brig we will only work one gang (a one-man gang, by the way). First we must find how many strakes of planking it will take to close her in, so measure the greatest girth at the midship frame from the edge of the lower top plank, now on, to the edge of the upper plank on the bottom. If the planking you have limits you to a certain width, divide the space in inches by the width of plank and see how many strakes it will make. But do not use too wide a plank. I would suggest eight inches and as the space is about 9 feet 4 inches (equal to 112 inches) this will give us 14 strakes.

Take a spiling, to determine the shape of the top edge of the next upper strake, and lay this out on a new plank to be cut. To determine how wide each strake must be, at various distances along its length, we make what is termed a planking scale. We don't really need this as yet as we could put on three or four strakes above and below by merely dividing the interval at, say, frame 7, forward, and 36, aft, into 14 planks and see how wide they should be there and then bend a batten to make a fair sweep for the lower edge of our strake we just spiled for.

But when the space has been thus narrowed down,

take a thin batten and measure on it the remaining
interval unplanked at the midship frame where the
plank are to be 8 inches wide and mark this point on
the batten 8. Then do the same at frame 7, and find
how wide the same number of plank must be to close
up the space there. For convenience we will say it

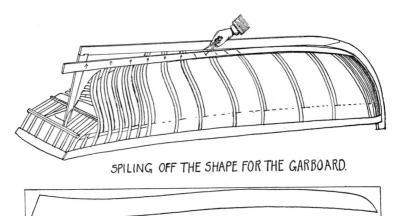

SPILING OFF THE SHAPE FOR THE GARBOARD.

THE SHAPE OF THE GARBOARD - LAID OUT ON A BOARD.

comes to an even 6 inches. Then mark that width on
your batten 6.

This batten is now made into a planking scale by
dividing up the space between the 6 and the 8, just as if
it were a part of a 2-foot rule, the 6 representing the
6-inch mark and the 8, the 8-inch. Halfway between
will be the 7-inch mark and half way between each
of these will represent the $6\frac{1}{2}$-inch, and $7\frac{1}{2}$-inch,
and halfway between each of these, again, will repre-
sent $\frac{1}{4}$-inch marks and so on down to $\frac{1}{8}$-inch or even
to $\frac{1}{16}$-inch.

To use this scale place the upper end against the
edge of the last top plank and amidships it will read
8 inches where it touches the bottom plank. So in

chalk mark 8 inches for the width of the plank at that
frame. Shift the scale forward two frames and it may
read 7⅛ inches, another two frames (intervals of two
frames will give you spots enough to draw a batten

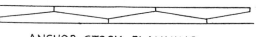

ANCHOR STOCK PLANKING.

line between them and lay out to shape of the un-
spiled edge of each plank), and it may read 7¾ and
so on until at frame 7 it will naturally register 6
inches. Mark the widths in chalk on each frame and
in getting out each plank it is obvious that if they are
made those widths at the respective frames, the space
will be evenly filled in with planking. Make a similar
scale for use from amidships aft.

The last plank to go on is called the "shutter." For
this you should use a narrow spiling plank and spile

TOP AND BUTT PLANKING.

off both edges to insure a tight fit. If we use full-
length planks, with no butts, as would be the case if
we had to use shorter lumber and make each strake of
planking in two or three pieces, we will avoid a lot of
trouble in laying out the butts so as not to cause a weak
spot by having these butt joints come too close to one
another.

Stringent rules govern this procedure in the shipbuilding trade. The essence of it may be found in the
following extract from the classification society's rules,
viz.: "No butts of adjoining plank should be nearer
each other than the space of three frames (when there

is a strake between them the distance of two frames will be allowed), and no butts to come on the same timber unless three strakes intervene." This is the American Bureau of Shipping rule while that of Lloyds is worded differently but produces substantially the same result: "No butts to be nearer than

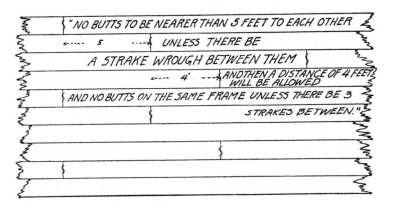

"NO BUTTS TO BE NEARER THAN 5 FEET TO EACH OTHER
5 UNLESS THERE BE
A STRAKE WROUGH BETWEEN THEM
4' AND THEN A DISTANCE OF 4 FEET WILL BE ALLOWED
AND NO BUTTS ON THE SAME FRAME UNLESS THERE BE 3
STRAKES BETWEEN."

SKETCH DESCRIPTIVE OF THE REQUIRED SHIFTING OF PLANK.
This sketch shows the principle on which the butts should be arranged, so as to avoid STEPPING, which is deemed bad workmanship. (from LLOYD'S)

5 feet to each other, unless there be a strake wrought between them, and then a distance of 4 feet will be allowed; and no butts to be on the same timber, unless there be three strakes between."

Remember that this book is written so that the amateur ship model builder can understand the rules of building and not become mentally swamped. It is a primer only and does not entitle the one who digests it, to a college degree. There are rules enough that have to be observed in the structure of a ship's hull, to fill two books like this. I have been at it all my life, as a business and as a hobby, but with all my books and experience of over forty years there is yet much that

I can learn. For instance, there are the rules for fastenings in a wood ship. Take the planking alone: plank 8 inches wide are to be single treenail fastened; plank 8 to 11 inches wide are to be double and single fastened, while all above 11 inches are to be double

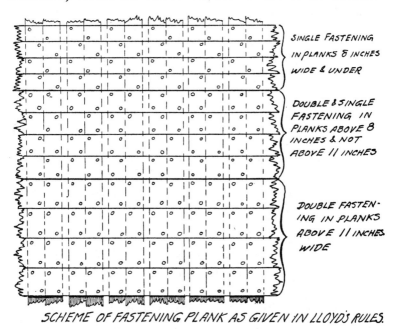

SINGLE FASTENING
IN PLANKS 8 INCHES
WIDE & UNDER

DOUBLE & SINGLE
FASTENING IN
PLANKS ABOVE 8
INCHES & NOT
ABOVE 11 INCHES

DOUBLE FASTEN-
ING IN PLANKS
ABOVE 11 INCHES
WIDE

SCHEME OF FASTENING PLANK AS GIVEN IN LLOYD'S RULES.

fastened. To explain this remember that each frame is made of two pieces, two futtocks, side by side. In single fastening there is one treenail near the top edge of the plank, into one futtock, and one near the bottom edge, into the other futtock. In double and single fastening there is a treenail in both top and bottom, into one futtock, and only one near the top in the second futtock. These are staggered so in the next frame there are two near the bottom (one in each futtock), and only one in the top edge of the plank.

In double fastening there are two fastenings in each

futtock, top and bottom. Every butt has to be secured with bolts; one driftbolt and one clinched through bolt. One of these may be in the adjoining timber to where the butt occurs. The butts come on a timber or frame and not on a butt-block between frames, as in small boat work.

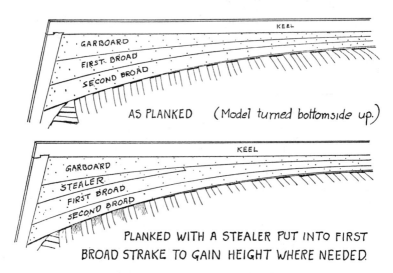

GARBOARD

FIRST. BROAD

SECOND BROAD

KEEL

AS PLANKED   (Model turned bottomside up.)

GARBOARD

STEALER.

FIRST BROAD.

SECOND BROAD

KEEL

PLANKED WITH A STEALER PUT INTO FIRST
BROAD STRAKE TO GAIN HEIGHT WHERE NEEDED.

Single fastening will do on all our planking except the wide hood ends in the garboard and broad strakes where there can be extra fastenings to compensate for the extra width. Use the ⅜-inch number 20 brads and finish off the whole surface of the planking with a flat file and then sand or use emery paper number 00 and finish off with a coat of linseed oil.

You will find you will have to resort to some home-made inventions or contrivances to get your planking on. On a real ship the same trouble occurs due to the fact that with the inside of the ship, planked up first, it is impossible to put a screw clamp in and hook it over a frame to draw the planking up snug. This is

overcome in actual practice by the use of specially
made clamps, such as a "toggle clamp" that can be
shoved in between two
frames. A hinged cross-
bar on it jams itself fast
when an outward pull is
put upon it. Another ex-
pedient is the "grass-
hopper jack" that can be
screwed into the face of
a frame and has a hinged
leg or brace out back that

A 12 x 14 INCH PIECE OF CLAMP STRAKE
BEING FORCED INTO SHAPE BY THE
USE OF SCREW CLAMPS AND RING STAFF
AND WEDGES.

jams and holds the jack in position as a strain is put upon the screw part of it. Other ship clamps, instead of a
pad foot, have a sharp claw-end that will dig in and

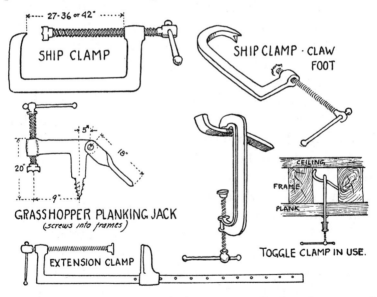

SHIP CLAMP

SHIP CLAMP · CLAW FOOT

GRASSHOPPER PLANKING JACK
(screws into frames)

EXTENSION CLAMP

TOGGLE CLAMP IN USE.

hold against the pull of the screw. So by the use of
these, ring staffs, chains and wedges, the various parts
of a ship are pulled into place to be fastened by bolts.

By not ceiling our little model all the way up inside, you can use small screw clamps but you will have to grind off the web so they are narrow enough to go in

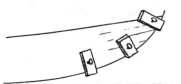

between the frames. Even then, to reach the garboard, I found I had to put a small piece of oak (some cuttings off the garboard)

HUTCHOCKS PREVENT SPLITTING

under the screw pad of the clamp, with one end on the place to be pulled down, and a small block of wood under the off end, to make a sort of lever out of it, because the clamp fitted so snug it could not be turned; the pressure had to be thus carried to the desired point. It worked finely and by clamps and wedges I jammed or "edge set" the garboard, snug into the rabbet along the keel, and fastened it off with $\frac{1}{2}$-inch number 20 brads, except away aft, at the heel, where the deadwood was so thin that even the $\frac{3}{8}$-inch brads came through and had to be snipped off and filed down.

You must be very careful at the forward end of the garboard, where it runs out to a point, and keep a thin slat of wood clamped over it to prevent its splitting. A good way is to bore for several fastenings along on this end and drive the brads you intend to use through

CAULKING SEAM ANGLE.

a piece of wood that will act as a pad, a hutchock, and pull on the surface of the garboard and it will not have a tendency to split, as the nail in the hole alone will do. This will hold the end as you fasten up to this point when, as you come to them, one by one, these pads can be split away and the brads driven home.

One good thing about it is that the model is now in

such shape that you can lift her out and hold her upside down on your lap while you put on the garboards and other plank; you don't have to get down under her and work up over your head, a back-break-ing job on the real ship.

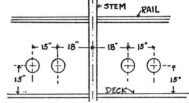

DISTANCE HAWSER-HOLES APART.

It will not be necessary to run a caulking edge on your plank, for if it is desired you can readily run a reamer along and compress the edges sufficiently. It is small enough on a full-sized ship, $\frac{1}{16}$-inch to every inch of plank thickness. The angle is readily deter-mined by opening the legs of a 2-foot rule, $\frac{5}{8}$-inch at the ends. This is just a trifle under the $\frac{1}{16}$ rule. The bevel is not generally carried clear to the back of the plank but only about two-thirds of the depth of the plank's edge.

The hawse holes, two on each side, can now be bored parallel with the center line of the ship, using a

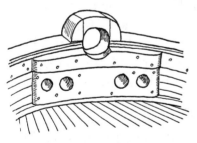

CHOCK FOR HAWSER HOLES

$\frac{1}{4}$-inch bitt which gives us an 8-inch diameter hole on the $\frac{3}{8}$-inch scale to which our model is built. They should center 15 inches above the deck. The first centers 18 inch-es away from the side of the stem and the second one 15 inches from the center of the first.

Under these work a black walnut bolster piece, its lower edge on a line with the top of the top plank or wale, its upper edge extending 3 inches above the bot-tom of the hawse hole and about 4 feet long. File a groove with a round file so it makes a round corner for the hawser as it comes out the hawse hole and goes down. This works a couple of grooves in this bolster piece. Butt this against the stem and round the outer corner and the upper edge.

We can now put on the knee of the head, or "head knee," for short. This, in a large ship, is built up of a

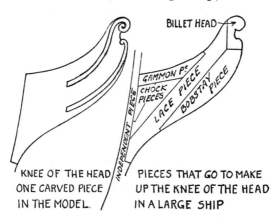

KNEE OF THE HEAD
ONE CARVED PIECE
IN THE MODEL.

PIECES THAT GO TO MAKE
UP THE KNEE OF THE HEAD
IN A LARGE SHIP

mass of timbers, the independent piece up parallel to and against the stem; from this, down below the water-line, a lace piece branches out forward, forming a V, the space between the two being filled in with chock pieces; and from this lace piece again branches out the bobstay piece, the curvature of the stem being worked in these two, the lace piece, the bobstay piece, and the gammoning piece on top of the chocks. But small vessels used a large knee or built it up of fewer pieces. We can cut ours out with a scroll saw from one piece of $\frac{5}{16}$-inch thick black walnut, but have the grain running diagonally at 45 degrees from the vertical.

I carved a billethead on my model's head knee. Whether you use that or wish to make it more decorative and put on a regularly carved image, is entirely optional with you. With figurehead or billethead the curved rails that radiate from the outer end run practically the same as they curve down and sweep aft merging into the cheeks, two stout knees that connect the head knee to the bows of the ship and brace it so it cannot be knocked sideways. The best way to cut these I have found is to make a cardboard pattern and after fitting it perfectly, then saw out a knee. Be sure to leave enough wood on the arm that fits against the hull, to cut the bevel. Cut it out of wood thick enough vertically to allow you to shape it with a slight upsweep to the outer end so it fairs in with the curve of the headrail that can be carved in relief on the head knee. Carve the billethead on the tip end and carry the rail back about an inch from the billet. From there cut the whole head knee from $\frac{5}{16}$ down to a stout $\frac{3}{16}$-inch and let the outer end of the cheek knees form the rest of the rail.

The forward edge of the knee of the head should be thinned down to $\frac{5}{32}$ of an inch and this edge, forming the cutwater, can be carried down to about the waterline and from there to the forefoot gradually come back to $\frac{1}{4}$-inch in thickness. The after ends of the cheek knees should form a line parallel to the rabbet line. If anything have the lower cheek knee a trifle longer than the upper cheek knee. Never make the upper cheek knee the longer.

Much of the beauty of your ship depends on the fairness in curvature and the symmetry with which the headrails are run, radiating from the billethead aft. Each rail should show a gradual increase in size as it comes aft and each space between the rails should likewise show a gradual increase in opening between the rails as you go aft. All should radiate like the leaves of a fan from a common center at the end of the billet-head.

The upper cheek knee is termed the hair bracket, as it is continued forward in an upward curve to the back of the billethead, or where the long flowing hair of a woman's head would be if the ship had a female for a figurehead.

To brace the extreme outer end of the knee of the head, a shore is fastened from the back of the billethead back to the cathead on the ship's bows. This is the mainrail, and according to the design of the ship had more or less sag or curvature to it, viewed from the side or sheer view, but it was a straight line if viewed from above.

Between these two ran a middle rail ending against the ship's side in more modern ships, but the farther back we go in the centuries, the more complex we find the disposition of these various rails of the head. William Sutherland gives us a good example of this in his book. In Plate VIII he gives the figurehead and rails as laid out in his day (1755) for a 1,000-ton ship carrying a lion for a figurehead. Here, a more elliptical effect is produced in the run of the headrails. Though the draughtsmanship is crude, the ideas expressed are those of a practical shipbuilder who gives us direct the meat in the cocoanut, even not forgetting the detail shapes of each rail. We find even then they were termed middle and lower rail and lace piece, and the general scheme was much the same. Three small brackets or head-timbers were fitted against the stem and knee of the head and resting on the top of the upper cheek knee and its rail continuation. The forward one raked the most, the one against the stem standing in rake with that member. The tops of these timbers supported the mainrail and the middle rail was notched into and also fastened to them.

Across the top of these timbers, faying against the after side of each, an arched beam, like a small deck beam, was fitted level with the toprail, across to the timber on the opposite side of the ship. Fore and aft pieces connected these beams and formed the framing for the seats of ease. Our little brig had the head-timbers but no crossbeams.

Fit the mainrail but do not fasten it in place. Using it as a guide, get out and fit in the three head-timbers on each side, and with a light batten, see that the middle rail will touch fair on all three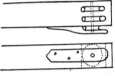

CAT-HEAD SHEAVES.

head-timbers and cut notches in them to receive it. When all are trued up then brad them fast permanently. A touch of glue at the joints will help hold them. Their outer ends should fit into small notches cut in the knee of the head to receive them, and at the after end the mainrail will butt against the forward side of the cathead, while the middle rail is carried aft and meets one that sweeps up under the cathead with a small knee finishing it off in a pretty sweep adding a very decorative finish to that part of the ship.

The cathead, itself, is a knee-like timber cut from a natural grained crook that is riveted on the inside of the bulwark to a framehead and extends three feet out from the ship's side, as a derrick on which to hoist up the anchor. In its outer end are to be cut two vertical scores to take 1-inch sheaves. The cathead should be 9 inches square at its outer end. On the forward side fit a chock, with a small brass sheave the same size as used in the sheaves of the cathead, their diameters being the same as the cathead is thick, viz.: 9 inches.

Under the cathead, on the outside of the ship, is a little knee to help support it, so small that it is the most difficult piece of wood in the whole ship to carve out,

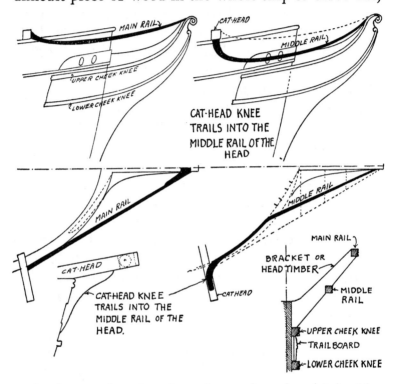

as it changes bevels where it touches the ship's side, and also sweeps forward in a quarter circle. When it is shaped it has one part at right angles to the other and is curled in like a twisted cow horn. Its forward end narrows down to the size of the middle rail. Another piece cut to fit the side and with a slight sweep continuing the fair curve of the rail, ends under the first bow-chase port, from where the rail in one piece goes to the end of the knee of the head. But you cannot put that part on until you have the top, the main-

rail, in place. This rail butts against the cathead knee
just at the rail and is cut with a sweep as shown on the
plans. Cut a notch in the back of the knee of the head
to form a landing for this rail so it comes in tangent to
the top scroll of the billethead. Then fit a wedge-
shaped chock or knee where these mainrails come to-

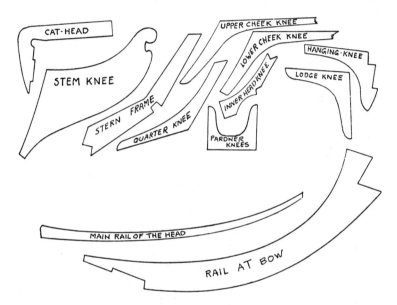

SOME OF THE PATTERNS USED IN BUILDING THE BRIG MODEL

gether. You will find it easier to fit and rivet in this
chock or knee before you fasten the rails to the hull;
but be sure you get them the right angle.

   With this rail in place, the head-timbers, three in
number, can be fitted in, making cardboard patterns
that flare in a straight line from the upper cheek knee
to the middle rail and from that one to the mainrail.
With these head-timbers in place you can see just what
shape the middle rail will take and where it will first
touch the side of the hull.

The inner head-timber, coming close to the hawse pipes, will have to be arched underneath so a towline will clear if pulled out straight ahead. The middle rail joins the hull just outside the end of the bolster pieces, under the hawse pipes, about two feet outside the outer hawse pipe. From there, aft to the cathead, it is plastered onto the outside planking of the ship.

The deck is now to be considered, whether to lay it complete or to leave some of it off so the beams and deck frame may be seen. Many of the old boxwood-built Admiralty models have only narrow strips of decking and most of the deck framing is exposed. In my little brig, however, I laid a full deck, to show all the guns and gun carriages, train tackles, breechings, etc., a deck being necessary, in from the bulwarks, far enough to take the gun carriages. This meant covering up the more important part of the deck frame with its lodge knees and hanging knees, so why leave the less important part exposed?

The deck changes the whole appearance of the model as she becomes a real little ship when it is all on. You can try laying it in individual strips if you prefer it so, but I did not go that far. I laid it in three strips to each side with short pieces down the center between the hatches. To do it this way, first plane down enough pine to the required thickness, sandpaper it and give it all a coat of orange shellac. When that is hard, polish it off lightly with very fine sandpaper. Then lay out the seams of the deck planking, I made mine 6 inches wide, and with a piece of round steel, ground down to a sharp point, using a straightedge as a guide, I scratched in a good seam about one-quarter the depth of the planking. Be careful or your scratch point will run with the grain. When so creased, you have broken through the thin glazing of shellac, and when you give the whole surface a coat of burnt umber the paint soaks into the seams. Help it do so with the paint brush, working the paint in thick. Then, after letting it set about five minutes, take a rag and rub off all the paint and your deck seams will stand out in black lines, clear and distinct, while the rest of the paint will all rub off the shellacked surface. If a white deck is desired, like a new, holystoned, bright-wood deck, then scrape off the shellac with a sharp wood scraper, after the paint in the seams has had a day or two to set.

The one difficulty of this method is in the nibbing strake or thin waterway. If laid, piece by piece, each deck plank's end can be nibbed off to a blunt point (about two inches or the width of a narrow caulking iron) and notches cut in the nibbing strake to receive them. Begin to plank such a deck at the side and work in toward the middle of the ship. To get this nibbing strake to show, by the other method, it is necessary first to fit the deck and then when you scratch in the seams, scratch the nib ends in after first carefully laying them out in pencil on the wood. The nibbing strake is then a part of these deck pieces and is not put in against the waterways, in a separate piece, as would be done if the deck were regularly laid.

The laid deck is almost impossible, as fastenings cannot be purchased small enough to be in proportion to the nails that would be used. It might be done in time and the heads punched in and plastic wood used to fill the holes in place of wood deck-plugs, but the spring of the unsupported span of the deck beams will surely cause you much trouble even if small bank pins or ¼-inch number 20 veneer brads be used for nails and you would have to edge-nail, as well, to keep the thin plank in alignment.

It is important to remember to first lay the decking down the center as wide as the hatchways, so you can fit in the bowsprit-bitts, bore the mast holes, etc., while the mast steps are still in sight and bore for and fit the pumps and the galley smokestack, "Charley Noble," as sailors facetiously nickname the latter. Our brig's bowsprit steps into a block of wood riveted in between the bitt posts. These two posts should go clear down and be let into or doweled at their foot into the ceiling. We cannot knee them fast so this is the best way of securing them against the thrust of the bowsprit. Build the bitts, let the bolster into the posts, and notch out the bolster a little also, riveting the bolster with a pin to each post. Then fit a block between the posts from the deck to the bolsters. Cut two holes through the reënforcing block between the third and fourth beams and set the bitts firmly in place. Cut the mast holes and pump holes, and then lay the rest of the deck. The after riding bitts, just abaft the foremast, can be put in later, after the deck is all on, but preferably now. Put the bitts together as you did the forward pair. Then with the bolster or cross piece on the afterside, cut a dovetail on the forward edge of the bitt posts that will let the ends just go through the decking and reënforcing block under it. Cut these holes just the size of the posts so you can get the big end of the dovetail down. Then drive a wooden wedge at the forward side of each post that will lock the dovetail securely. Touch the wedge into glue and then cover it over by fitting in the knes that strengthen each set of bitts against the pull of the anchor cables.

The hull at this point being practically completed,

the work that follows is the small detail that may, if
one so wishes, consume a great deal of time. It is from
this point that many men most enjoy the work of model
making. In taking great pains to make every little
detail a hundred per cent perfect supplies a most en-
joyable occupation that takes one's mind completely
from the daily grind of life. It is a hobby, a pastime,
in which men get a complete change of thought and
it has the lure of the romance and adventure that sailing ships always awaken in a man. He rebuilds small
replicas of such ships as his forefathers may have
fought in while achieving the freedom of the United
States or ventured into foreign seas on mercantile en-
terprises. Every little detail can be dug up by research
and in doing so one broadens his vision of the world by
finding out many quaint practices that were indulged
in by the old timers, the hardships they endured, the
crude implements with which they worked, and their
own quaint customs and ideas.

How would you live on such a craft as this? Consider what you would want and then limit yourself to
what was in those days obtainable. A study as to how
drinking and cooking water was carried, how the bar-
rels of beef, pork and hard-tack were stowed, how the
powder and cannon balls and huge cables were stowed
away leaving room for about a hundred men to sleep
and live is all most interesting, but in our model we
will confine our study to such as concerns only the
things above deck.

Enough will be found here to satisfy almost any
man. Let us enumerate some of these details. There is
the rudder, its gudgeons and pintles, its tiller, and the
reënforced head where the tenon of the tiller cuts
away part of the wood; the key that holds the tiller in

tight; the binnacle in which the compass was kept; the cavils and mooring ports where ropes could be passed ashore to hold the brig alongside a dock; the port shutters and hinges, capstan, capstan bars, and how and where the latter were kept handy for use. There was the messenger, a rope wrapped several turns around the capstan and then lead out around the bitts and mast to the bows where, away up in the eyes of her, under the bowsprit, a sheave or a big snatch block, hooked to an eyebolt, was ready to reeve it over. The end was then brought aft on the other side and the two ends of the messenger seized together so it made an endless loop and by several frappings put about it and the huge hemp cables, too big and stiff to bend around the barrel of the capstan, brought these cables in and with them the anchors of 500 to 800 pounds in weight. The channels, chain plates and deadeyes, the pinrails and all the many belaying pins; the pumps and the sounding pipe and rod to measure the depth of water in the ship's bottom; the location of the ship's bell, scuttle butt for drinking water, galley smoke pipe, scuppers to carry water from the deck overboard; all these fittings and the small boats and their davits, the hammock nettings, gun ports, hinges, lanyards and so on and so on, to say nothing of the cannon, gun carriages, breechings, train tackles, in-hauls, rammers, sponges, shot racks and the hundred or more little ringbolts for all the gun tackles to hook into,—all these require attention.

It is in getting this detail to scale and in correct appearance, that gives a model a true shippy look or the appearance of a toy boat. Be careful to keep everything to scale. Do not have cannon balls stowed in the shot racks that are many sizes too big for the bore of the cannon. Keep at it until you get the right size shot.

I always cut out the figure of a man, to scale, and set him around any fitting I am making, to see if it is the right height for a man to work the pump handles, capstan bars, etc., and I find it a help in checking up on the scale as it also helps to visualize the deck furniture.

The rudder's shape is shown on the plans. It is cut out of black walnut the same thickness as the keel and sternpost, tapered to $\frac{1}{8}$-inch at the after edge and reduced slightly on the forward edge near the lower end. The forward edge, below the deck level, is chamfered off on the edges. The gudgeons and pintles by which it is hinged to the sternpost now start us into making ironwork. An ink bottle filled with alcohol, with a short piece of thin brass tubing through the cork, and a round wick, is all one needs to do the soldering by which the ironwork can be made. A piece of heavy copper wire stuck into a piece of wood, for a handle, makes a good soldering iron and a small can of soldering paste can be bought, as well as solder.

There are three pair of gudgeons and pintles to be made out of thin sheet brass or copper. Cut it with scissors into strips $\frac{3}{32}$-inches wide. Bend it around a large pin or piece of brass wire the size the pintles are to be (a scant $\frac{1}{16}$-inch in diameter), then holding this pin in place, bend the rest of the strip so it fits snug around the rudder keeping the pintle or pin close to the rudder. Now solder the pin in place by first putting a tiny bit of the flux, or soldering paste, where the pin is and heating it in the flame until it melts and runs in around the parts to be soldered. Then touch the strip of solder to this spot, holding it in the flame until the solder runs in all around the pin and then take it away and let it cool. The gudgeons are made the same way only there is no pin. The solder may fill the hole but that can be easily bored out afterwards to take the pintle. The solder will stiffen the fittings and can be filed down to a finish. Bend the two strips until they will fit flush into a score cut into the rudder and into the sternpost. Set the pintles and gudgeons at right angles to the forward edge of the rudder and rivet them through on each side. Keep the gudgeon eye close to the sternpost and let the pintle straps into the forward edge of the rudder until the pintle pin is in a direct line with the edge of the rudder. To ship the rudder, gouge out a small recess behind and under each pintle, but keep the rudder as close up to the sternpost as it will go and still turn. The object is to prevent leaving a wide crack through which the water from the lee side will squirt through when the ship is heeled over and pressing against it, as that lessens the efficiency of the rudder as a turning agent for the ship. Moreover, it looks better when fitted up close.

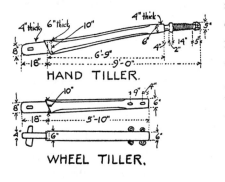

HAND TILLER.

WHEEL TILLER.

Many of the little brigs of the size of the *Lexington* steered with a tiller and so I fitted this model with a 9-foot one. Here was where my dummy man came into use so as to get the tiller about waist high or 3 feet 3 inches from the deck to the center of the ball carved on the tiller's end. Cut with an S-shaped sweep morticed through the rudderhead the tiller was left square-edged at the rudderhead. The corners were then chamfered, becoming octagonal near the end where, between two raised ridges, there was a narrow groove left where the grommet, with two eyes to hook relieving tackles into, was kept from sliding. From there to the ball on the tiller's end, was a slightly tapered round handle that I served with fine black thread to make a good hand grip for the helmsman. The tenon on the tiller extended out back of the rudderhead, just far enough to permit a small wooden, wedge-shaped key to be driven horizontally through it. The rudderhead was reënforced by two thin cheeks of black walnut, riveted through with pins for rivets.

If you put a steering wheel on your model this tiller can be made shorter by several feet and kept lower on the forward end, but don't get it so low that it will hit the deck when the rudder swings hard over to 45 degrees. Make the tiller of hard wood. I found the black walnut excellent for this purpose and, in fact, for all small stuff such as the headrails, cheek knees, cat heads, tiller, binnacle, and hatch coamings. It gives a much better appearance to the model to keep to a wood of the same color. At first I made my rudder stock of walnut; a parallel piece of ¾-inch in width, down where the rudder blade came, and built out the other ¾-inch with a piece of oak bradded on. But the contrast in color was great as soon as the linseed oil, with which I liberally soaked each piece of new work, darkened the stock more than the oak, so I removed the latter and built out the rudder blade again with another piece of black walnut causing it to look very much better.

This short tiller should have a couple of wires horizontally through its end, or near its end, turned into eyes on each side into which the tiller-tackles are to be hooked with two ringbolts in the deck on each side to hook the outer blocks to. The hauling ends of these tackles can then be led to a couple of single blocks hooked into eyebolts directly under the barrel of the steering wheel, or led forward from the outer blocks to a block on each side parallel to the center line of the ship until opposite or abreast the middle of the spool or barrel of the steering wheel and from there come in and around the barrel. While it takes up a little more deck room the latter has a longer lead to the barrel and so a better chance to lay around the barrel without having one turn or fake ride up over the next one and jamb. This is as I rigged it on the model.

The proper location for these outer blocks, in the tiller-tackles, has always been a much argued point. The aim is to give the least slack to the rope as the tiller sweeps across the deck from hard-a-starboard to hard-a-port. In so doing its end describes an arc of a circle and the outer block should be half way, in a fore-and-aft direction, between the two extremes, between the point where it stands amidships and when hard over, only the outer block must be out a couple of feet beyond the point where the end of the tiller is when hard over. There will be less slackening of the tiller ropes at this point than anywhere else the block can be hooked.

Do not splice the end of the tiller ropes to the blocks. Clinch with a half knot, and then stop the end down with thread. This is done with marlin on a real ship and permits the ready taking up of slack as the ropes stretch. The old timers used raw hide, when they could get it, and that could not be spliced but had to be stopped.

Even with the tiller we have to fit tackles but these

were only temporary, for use in a stiff breeze of wind, and hooked into eyes in the becket around the tiller and then to ringbolts in the bulwarks or eyebolts in the deck out near the waterway. The ringbolts were preferable as eyebolts in the deck are mean things to stub your toe against on a dark night.

To make a steering wheel is a jeweler's job. The hardest part is to make the hub. This would be about 6 inches in diameter in the real ship and on a $\frac{3}{8}$-inch scale model it means $\frac{3}{16}$ of an inch. This hub can either be a solid piece of $\frac{3}{16}$-inch brass rod $\frac{1}{8}$-inch thick, with the socket holes bored around its edge, or the ends of the spokes can be left large enough so their eight ends fit together for a solid center and the hub be made of two small discs with a pin rivet through each. There is nothing complicated about this but it is very fine work to make a neat job of it. With a small lathe the spokes can be accurately turned out of boxwood, making a very handsome wheel.

The wheel should be about 4 feet 6 inches in diameter and the handle ends should be 6 inches long. Just inside the handles or "spokes," rivet a circle of thin brass, on each side, and fit in an arc of wood between these brass circles, from spoke to spoke, putting two pin rivets in each arc piece. Round the edges of these pieces so they show a scant $\frac{1}{32}$ of an inch beyond the $\frac{3}{32}$ of an inch wide brass rims or circles. When it is all together drill a hole in the center of the hub for the shaft, working it into a square hole with a square rat-tailed file, one in the "die sinker" set of files that you can buy and should have if you intend to make models.

The stand for the steering wheel was built in a great variety of shapes and consisted of a support at each end of the horizontal steering wheel shaft. The wheel was generally just forward of the forward support or stand-ard, with the spool or barrel between the two standards. These supports of an A-shape or inverted V, were generally at each end although sometimes the after one or the forward one, was a single upright.

The next job we should tackle is to fit and hang the port shutters. Some of the small craft, like our brig, did not have hinged port lids but shutters that were put in place by hand and held there by lashings or port bars. Others had what were termed half-ports and bucklers, the lower half of the shutter being hinged at the bottom and the upper half a loose piece fitted in place by hand and then held there. The upper edge fitted into a rabbet to receive it as did the lower edge where it fitted into a ledge cut in the top of the lower half of the shutter, — the hinged piece. By heaving on the lanyard, by which the lower half was closed, the upper half was forced snug into its rabbets by being "buckled," as it was termed, and from which term the upper, loose half of the port shutter received the name of "the buckler." This form of a port shutter was generally cut out so it left a round hole (half in each piece of the port shutter) that fitted snugly around the cannon, which were left run out, and a "tompion," as the plug was called, fitted into the muzzle of the gun to keep out the salt sea water.

Vessels having several decks carrying cannon, generally had solid, one-piece port shutters on the lower deck ports, and half shutters, or two-piece ones, on the other upper deck ports. The upper half was raised by means of a tackle hooked to the side of a deck beam above the gun port. This was connected to a small chain that went out through a small hole bored through the ship's side and was shackled to an eyebolt in the lower

end of the strap hinge on the port shutter. The lower
half was simply knocked out, its lower edge being
hinged, and the upper edge dropped to a horizontal
position where it was stopped by a small chain on each
side, shackled to eyebolts in the side of the porthole.

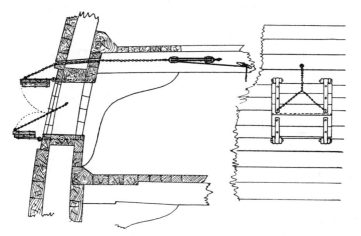

DETAILS OF A GUN·PORT

In order to be able to load the cannon, when run in
with the ports still closed, there was a small round hole
with a moveable shutter, just to keep water out, on the
outside of the solid shutter, cut in the center, to allow
the handle of the ramrod to be run out through it. Just
above this was another, called the "illuminator," which
was in line with the gun sights so the enemy's ship
might be seen while the port was still closed. These
were necessary on covered decks but on an open deck,
with nothing but the sky above, such fittings to the port
lids were not needed.

The port shutters should be fitted first. The bulwarks ending about $\frac{1}{32}$ of an inch back from the edge
of the frame forming the port and the sill about the

same height above the planking of the bulwarks so as to form a slight rabbet for the port shutters to stop against. When all the port shutters are snugly fitted, make and put on the hinges. I timed myself and found I could make the hinges and hang one port shutter in 24 minutes. I took a piece of paper-thin, shim brass,

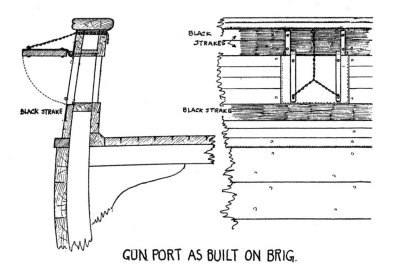

GUN PORT AS BUILT ON BRIG.

and cut off a strip, a stout $\frac{1}{16}$-inch in width. I bent the end of this over an ordinary sized pin (about 1 inch in length) and after pinching the brass with tweezers close against the pin and turning it back just far enough to form an eye, I had enough left to drill a hole through the two thicknesses to hold a small $\frac{1}{2}$-inch bank pin. Leaving the big pin in place I laid this partially made strap hinge on the port shutter, so the big pin and the eye it went through were even with the top of the shutter and parallel $\frac{1}{16}$-inch in from the vertical edge of the shutter. Then I drilled a hole through the two thicknesses of brass and the wooden shutter and inserted a bank pin that just drove snug through this hole with the pin's head against the brass, which, I forgot to say, I reamed lightly with a larger drill enough to remove the square edge and let the pinhead fit snug against the brass.

Turning the shutter over I snipped off the pin with cutting pliers, close to the wood, gave a few strokes across it with a fine file to make the pin end rivet better,

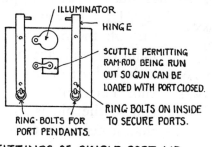

RING·BOLTS FOR PORT PENDANTS.

FITTINGS OF SINGLE PORT LID

and then, tapping very lightly, riveted the pin end. Then snipping off the head of a bank pin I turned a small eye on it and drilling another hole through the brass strip, about $\frac{1}{8}$-inch from the lower edge of the port shutter, reamed the hole lightly and drove the eyepin through, cut it off and riveted it. This operation was repeated until both strap hinge parts were on the shutter, being careful to keep them parallel with the edge of the shutter and each other.

The same kind of eyes were again turned in brass over another pin, only now the holes were bored and reamed, but the holes in the straps were only $\frac{3}{16}$ of an inch apart, as the hinge part there was only a total length of $\frac{1}{4}$ inch. Two of these were made, the big pin then withdrawn, and one of these short straps inserted on the pin. It was then put back through the long strap eyes on the shutter and the other short strap put on the pin. I should here call attention to the fact that in each case the short end of each strap hinge part was put under and against the wood, so that the end was covered. Put the port shutter back in place, raise the short straps up against the outer rail stringer, bore holes and drive in bank pins cut off to only about ³⁄₁₆-inch in length and filed again to a sharp point and the port is hung, but not finished. The big pinhead is un-

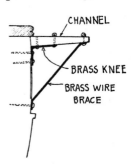

sightly, so take another big pin and snip off the head and hold it in a hand vise and tapping lightly, raise a slight burr or head on the heavy end. Then cut off the sharp point end so the pin is ¹⁄₁₆-inch longer than is necessary to go through the strap hinges and round the end with a file and pulling out the first pin insert this one in its place and your port hinge is complete. With the two bow ports and two stern ports and eight ports on each side there are twenty pairs of such hinges to make and put on.

Of course there are other ways of hanging port lids or shutters. Some ships did not have the long pin or bar, but only a short stub riveted or welded into the eye of the long strap so it was like a pintle and gudgeon on a rudder. Others had two eyes instead of the upper short strap, one each side of the eye in the long strap, and then had short bolts through them.

The channels are made of a hard wood. I used black walnut. They are 18 inches in width and 4 inches thick and extend aft from about opposite the masts, for a length of 12 feet. They just clear the ports at their forward ends and go over the top of one port, being abutted against the outer rail stringer just under the mainrail. They are carried as shown, so that a bolt may be put through a framehead close to each end of the channel, with two intermediate ones. Bore clear through the channel and drive long, slim brads into the heads of the timbers. But before you do this make two brass or copper knees and rivet them to the underside of the channel so they will lay against and can be fas-

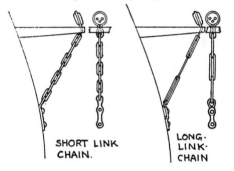

SHORT LINK CHAIN.

LONG·LINK·CHAIN

tened to the outer planking at a frame. The outer rivet to these knees make into an eye on top of the channel for halliard blocks to hook into.

The inner edge of the channel will have to be scribed and shaped to fit fair on the fore-and-aft curvature of the ship's side. The channel should stand out horizontally from the hull and be held securely by a stout wire brace with an eye in each end screwed fast under the channel near its outer edge, about midlength, with a round-headed brass nail holding the lower end just above the plank-sheer.

The channels should be about 5 inches thick at the hull and 4 inches on the edges. Notches should be cut in the outer edge to receive the chain plates or deadeye strappings and when all are on, a light moulding is put along the outside to finish off the appearance of the edge. You will notice in all future fittings the necessity of so placing them that fastenings may be had into either the deck beams, if it be a deck attachment, or into a frame of the ship, as in the case of chain plates and channels. You cannot just put them on anywhere, as is the case in a carved out block model.

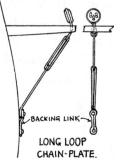

BACKING LINK
LONG LOOP
CHAIN-PLATE.

To locate the position and angle of the chain plates, now that you have the actual hull and do not have to work it out on a plan, put a stick in the mast hole and fasten a piece of cord to it the height of the trestletrees upon the masthead where the shrouds would lead from, and lead this string down over the edge of the channel to the ship's side and set it so you can get bolts to go into the frames. Mark thus the location of the lower shrouds as shown in the rigging plan. The topmast and other backstays can be laid out the same way and all the chain plates put on at once if you want to complete that part of the job now. Then brad on a light strip of half round along the edge to hold all the chain plates in place.

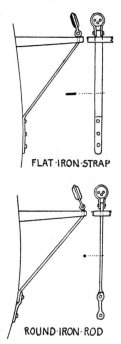

FLAT-IRON-STRAP

ROUND-IRON-ROD

The kind of chain plates used on a model should be carefully selected as to period and location, as Maine-built ships and New York- or Philadelphia-built vessels had differences in the character of their iron work by which a sea captain could often tell where the ship was built without seeing her name. In the olden days chains were used, then a few long links somewhat resembling a chain came into use, then round iron rods, square rods, and flat iron straps followed. It was their remoteness from the iron mills that caused the far-away Maine shipyards to cling to the use of rod iron when the shipyards farther south began using flat strap iron.

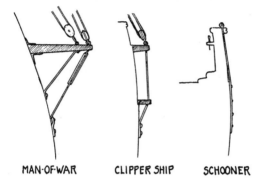

MAN-OF-WAR   CLIPPER SHIP   SCHOONER

The shape and character of the ship, whether a wall-sided clipper or a heavily tumbled-home, topsided, old sailing man-of-war, had a good deal to do with the kind of channels and chain plates used. A large frigate or ship-of-the-line, with a deck or two above her main deck and the point of greatest beam, had to have channels wide enough for men to walk on in order to spread her lower shrouds so as to clear the hammock nettings on her top-rail, and these channels were placed at the main deck level. They were huge platforms and had to be supported and steadied by knees and braces. On the other hand, a sleek, smooth-sided clipper ship, with only bulwarks above her main deck, only needed channels wide enough to have the deadeyes and lanyards clear of the rail. They became mere battens on the side of the ship, offering far less resistance when the ship was heeled. The old-fashioned wide channels and chain plates tore the water into an arc of white foam when the ship heeled down.

For effecting quick repairs, the bolts on the lower ends of the chain plates were made flat one way, on French men-of-war, and the chain-plate end had a slot so that by turning the bolt head vertically the chain plate could be removed. By giving the bolt head a half

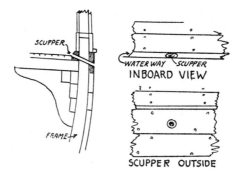

turn the shoulders of the bolt head straddled the chain plate and held it securely.

Round rod iron was the fashion in the days when the *Lexington* was built, made into long links. The dead-eye strapped with the same and a short reënforcing link, known as a backing link, permitted another fastening to the hull below the first bolt. This was the prevailing custom at the time of the Revolution.

There is one small item which on account of its apparent insignificance is often overlooked by model builders, and that is the deck scuppers. At the lowest point of the deck, as the ship rides on an even keel at anchor, where rain water would lodge on the deck, lead pipes are fitted that go out through the side of the ship down about a strake or two from the deck level. Forward and aft of this spot others are put in as the ship may not always be trimmed to set on the water to exactly the same level and also because, as she heels, the lowest point may be forward of this first scupper. Three or four scuppers on each side are sufficient. I could not get lead pipe small and thin enough and a small brass or copper tube does not look natural and stares at you like a sore thumb. I used some lead foil, such as comes around some kinds of tobacco. It was about as thick as a sheet of stout paper. I rolled it about three times around a round stick about the size of a match and, after boring a hole from the water- way in the corner made by the deck and bulwark, aimed so that the bitt came out through the top plank on the outside of the hull *between two frames,* I worked this stick with the foil on it (the edge being lightly soldered down smooth) through this hole. I had lightly reamed the edges of the holes and after trimming off the little lead scupper pipe made from leadfoil, I gently expanded each end of this scupper so it looked true to life. It showed a flange on the inside and it was flush with the planking on the outside. It should come through a plank somewhere near its middle and not in a seam. It would look badly in a seam, for they never came there, so be careful to see you hit the middle of the plank.

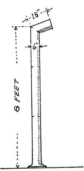

"CHARLIE NOBLE"
GALLEY SMOKE PIPE.

A formal occasion in the lives of all novices aboard a man-of-war was their introduction to the warm- hearted, brave "Charley Noble." This ceremony was gravely carried out by the older members as they marched their victim about the ship to finally stop him before the galley smoke pipe—that was Charley Noble. The range, with its great coppers for boiling the crew's messes, was on the deck below and on our little brig the smoke pipe comes up through a metal ring in the deck and stands up about nine feet above it, with a bent elbow on the end. Two brass grommets, the long shank kind used in aeroplane work, made me a stack about 5 inches in diameter, soldered together with another short piece for the elbow. Roll some thin sheet brass and solder the seam and you can make a pipe if you haven't anything ready-made that you can use.

Men-of-war generally did not have a continuous pin-rail running the whole length of the bulwarks, as was the custom on merchant ships. The guns and gun ports interfered with such an arrangement and more gear was rove so it came inboard to the fore and main bitts and some of the uppermost gear stopped in the fore and main tops which, being always manned, was belayed there and handled by these men. A little brig of this size would have a midshipman and eight men in a top when reefing and hoisting sail. A different number would be there in various other manoeuvers.

But abreast each mast there were a certain number of ropes that had to go out to the rail and so on our brig we will fit in a pinrail between the guns in the slightly wider space at the rigging. This rail would be just under 8 feet in length and 9 inches wide by 3 inches thick. It would be fastened to the inner rail stringer, just above its lower edge, with slim brads into each framehead. On each side of the bowsprit fit a pinrail 4 feet in length to take the belaying pins on which are belayed the jib-downhauls and all other running gear that leads inboard at this point. Instead of a belaying pin, on account of the thickness of the fore and main sheets, a large cleat or cavil was usually provided for belaying sheets to and so we have fitting a long cavil on the inside of our bulwarks for this purpose, just forward of where the sheave is fitted in the ship's side for the sheet to reeve through. These sheaves are a very important part of the ship's equipment and make a picturesque touch that sets off a model's appearance wonderfully. It's just such little things as this that makes one model stand out from among a lot of others where such details have been neglected as being unimportant.

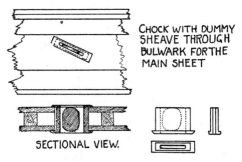

CHOCK WITH DUMMY SHEAVE THROUGH BULWARK FOR THE MAIN SHEET

SECTIONAL VIEW.

I cut through the bulwarks and waist and fitted in a solid block of black walnut cut with a thin shoulder that fetched up against the bulwarks outside and stopped its going through and made a neat finish on the outside. Then another thin flat piece was fitted over the end of this block after it was cut flush with the inside of the waist, for it went clear through both bulwark outside and waist inside and had a hole bored clear through it for the sheet to reeve through. The end pieces were bored and filed with a rat-tail file to represent a sheave. Such sheaves should also be provided for the fore-sheets. An eyebolt in the outside of the ship, just above the plank-sheer moulding, about two frames space forward of the sheave, is where the standing end of the mainsheet shackles fast. Spreading it thus prevents its fouling by frapping or twisting of the two parts together.

The fore-sheet is similarly treated, only, in order to keep it from getting afoul of the gun muzzles, the sheave is kept up higher, being put through the outer and inner rail stringers and the eyebolt for the standing end the same. The courses for the big, lower square sails were, on account of these sheets and tacks coming down in the way of the guns, generally clewed up when

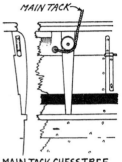

MAIN TACK CHESSTREE

a ship went into action. The tacks, as the ropes by which the forward corners of the courses, forecourse and maincourse or foresail and mainsail, as they were termed by some sailors, led, in the case of the main, in a similar way through a sheave in the bulwark abaft the fore channels. As it came down almost vertically from the sail, it had to have a vertical sheave to reeve over before it went through the horizontal sheave hole in the bulwarks. This sheave was set in a short vertical timber, termed a chesstree, which you will find indicated on most old plans, bolted fast on the outside of the ship's bulwarks.

In the case of the foretack, the conditions are very different. Owing to the foremast being so far forward on old-time ships, the corner or clew of the forecourse, when the foreyard was braced around for the ship to sail close hauled, pointing as close up into the wind as she could sail, came out beyond the bows of the ship. In order to pull this forward edge of the sail tight, a short, stout spar called a bumpkin, had to be fitted, that projected diagonally out from the ship's bow so its outer end came under and a little beyond this corner of the sail. With a block toggled into the clew of the forecourse and another stropped around the end of the bumpkin, a tackle, called the foretack, was rove off and the hauling end led inboard through a hole in the bulwarks.

On the high-bowed frigates and other larger ships, this bumpkin had guys to help support it; one led forward to the edge of the knee of the head; one led down to an eyebolt in the ship's bows and yet kept clear of the ground tackle, as the anchors and cables were called;

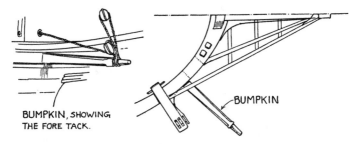

BUMPKIN, SHOWING
THE FORE TACK.

BUMPKIN

and another led aft to an eyebolt. Care has to be exercised to see that none of this conflicts with the working of any other part of the ship's gear, which statement applies to every part of a ship's outfit. See that everything is workable and practical. On small craft like our brig, a lower bumpkin guy would be in the way of the anchor cable, in catting and stowing the anchor. So in our case a heavier bumpkin must be provided, one stout enough to stand the pull of the foretack alone and unsupported. This means a bumpkin about 8 inches square where it comes through the bulwarks and a tenon cut on its end is let into a square hole cut for it in the bow timbers. The bumpkin is tapered to 6 inches at the end with a shoulder formed about 6 inches from the outer end to stop the grommet and strop about the tack blocks from sliding inboard, and just above it put a tiny tube through the bows for the hauling end of this tack-tackle to lead through, with a large cleat for it to belay on, on the inside of the bulwarks. The corners of the bumpkin are chamfered so it is octagonal just inside the shoulder.

The main tack on these old-time ships did not lead as on modern ships. On American merchant ships in the 1890's, when I went to sea, both sheets and tacks

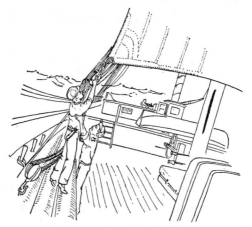

HOOKING THE MAIN TACK TACKLE.

were unhooked when the course was clewed up, and only a single heavy rope, called a "tail rope," spliced into the clew iron of the sail, was left to go up with the sail. In setting a course, as the clew line was slacked away, a couple of hands hauled down on this tail rope. All hands in the deck watch then hauled it down until the heavy tackle block could be lifted up and the big iron hook, as thick as your wrist, hooked into the clew iron in the lower corner of the sail. In light airs this clew iron could be hauled close down quite easily, but in heavy winds sometimes all hands could not get the clew of the sail down so a man standing on deck could reach it. A ship's deck is a swaying, pitching platform on which to balance one's self and hold up, at arm's length, a block with ropes that was all a strong man could lift. I have shinned up the tail rope while the mate and a seaman tried to hold up this clumsy tack-tackle so I could engage the hook into the clew iron, and sometimes we have struggled for ten minutes before we could get the tack-tackle hooked.

In the case of the foretack, which came down to a ringbolt on the cathead about at the rail, this was taken around the capstan on the forecastle and the foretack was hove down, "boarded," as the term is. The main-tack came down inside of the bulwarks, the tack-tackle having its upper block hooked into the clew of the sail and its lower, a becket block, being hooked into a stout ringbolt in the ship's waterways or covering boards. No capstan being handy, down here in the low part of the ship's deck, in the waist, a luff tackle was clapped onto the hauling part, a rope strop was wound tightly around the rope, then the lower bight or loop of the strop was taken up and passed through the upper bight, the pull being down, so the pull on this bight jammed the strop so it would not slip down or "ride home." The additional power this luff tackle gave, pulled the tack-tackle taut enough to straighten out the weather luff of the main course to the mate's satisfaction. Several times in heavy weather, a man was sent to the carpenter shop, a narrow room in the forward deckhouse between the galley aft and the crew's forecastle in the forward end, to get a snatch block. This was hooked into a ringbolt in the deck or waterways and the luff tackle fall, its hauling end, was taken up to the capstan on the raised poop deck that began just aft of the mainmast. To reach this distance a messenger had to be used. A messenger is merely an extra piece of rope tied on to the fall to lengthen it out so it will reach the capstan, but in hitching two ropes together to stand such a strain and yet not jamb so tightly as to be unable to quickly be untied, is where one learns a bit of seamanship.

The leeward clews have the sheets hooked into them, a mousing put on the bill of the hook so it cannot shake off, and the sheets hauled in as taut as the mate's judgment decides it should be. There being only two parts to the sheet, this necessarily has to be quite a heavy rope to stand the strain put upon it. One end is hooked and moused or shackled into an eyebolt in the outside of the ship's planking at about the deck level. It reeves

A MOUSEING ON A HOOK
"HOOK END ALWAYS HAS A
NIB END TO HOLD SEIZING
FROM SLIPPING OFF "

up through the big, single block hooked into the clew of the sail, then aft through a bee-hole in the ship's bulwarks, reeving over a big sheave built in to take it, and comes out on the inside where, it being too big a rope to belay on a belaying pin, a cavil is provided over which it may be hitched or taken around a mooring bitt generally located near by for making breast lines fast to when the ship is tied up to a wharf.

The fore-sheet comes through the bulwarks over a sheave similar to that of the mainsheet only, located between two gun ports as it is, there is not room for so long a cavil as at the main, belaying on a cleat on the inside of the bulwark. Small as these fittings are collectively, they give the otherwise barren hull a shippy, finished look. Every little item of deck furniture adds its quota.

The binnacle set up on deck just in front of the tiller's end was the old box type, a rectangular box sup-

ported on four wooden legs cleated fast to the deck.
This was built with a compartment on each end in
which a lamp could be set by opening a little hinged
door at each end, with a compass in the central compartment. In the subdividing partitions, round holes,
covered with glass, permitted the lamp light to shine

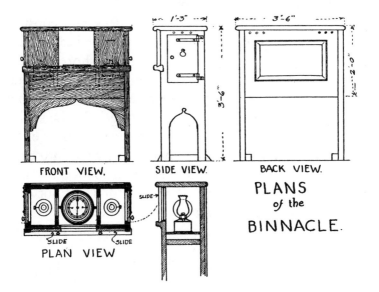

FRONT VIEW.   SIDE VIEW.   BACK VIEW.

PLANS
of the
BINNACLE.

PLAN VIEW

through illuminating the compass without throwing a
blinding glare into the helmsman's eyes. Anyone who
has ever steered a craft at night can appreciate the im-
portance of this. A little round peephole, only half an
inch in diameter, was bored through each door and covered with a pivoted flap, by pushing aside which the
deck officer could see if the lamp were burning or not
and yet the flap prevented a tell-tale ray of light being
seen by the enemy as it hung down by its own gravity
and closed this peephole. Small holes near the top let
out the heat and smoke of the lamp. The compass face
could, when necessary, be screened by sliding doors that

closed it. This binnacle stood 3 feet 6 inches off the deck to its top on which was fastened a small brass bell hung on an arch-shaped bracket on which the man at the wheel struck the hours and half-hours every time he turned the sand glass. The box-like top was 3 feet 6 inches wide, athwartships, 1 foot 3 inches fore and aft, and 2 feet deep, exclusive of the legs.

Before we go forward along her deck and consider the other fittings maybe you will be tempted to do what I did. Considering that she was an off-shore craft, a deep-waterman, I decided to have pity on her helmsman and fit her with a steering wheel. You cannot buy the proper kind of a wheel, but having held the spokes of one of these critters for hours on end, I knew every rivet and piece of wood and metal that went into their make-up, so went up to my workshop room and made up a wheel, a rough one, I'll admit, for I did not even have a small lathe to turn out the spokes, as I should have liked to, or the means of spinning out the metal rims.

The way I did it was this. The wheel was to be 4 feet 8 inches in diameter over the ends of the spokes. This is 56 inches and three times this gives us a circumference of 168 inches. A reach between spokes of 21 inches $(168 \div 21 = 8)$ gives us a wheel of eight spokes. Allowing 6 inches for the length of the spoke end, the handgrips, gives 3 feet 8 inches for the diameter of the brass rim which I made 3 inches wide, and the reach between spokes at the rim $16\frac{1}{2}$ inches. Not having the means of spinning these two brass rims out of hard brass, I had to take some thin sheet brass I could cut with very small, sharp-pointed scissors, and cut them out by hand. I marked the shape out, $1\frac{1}{4}$-inches diameter, with a pair of dividers, scratching the circle on the brass, and $\frac{3}{32}$ of an inch inside of this line I swept the inner circle. It was difficult to cut so narrow a rim as the scissors tended to buckle the brass but it made quite a passable job when done. For the hub I cut out two small circles or discs of the same brass, $\frac{1}{4}$-inch in diameter, representing about 8 inches in the model. Then to make the spokes I planed up some small ash

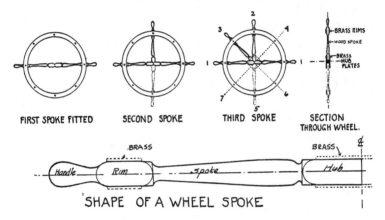

FIRST SPOKE FITTED   SECOND SPOKE   THIRD SPOKE   SECTION THROUGH WHEEL.

SHAPE OF A WHEEL SPOKE

sticks, a stout $\frac{1}{16}$-inch square. A 12-inch strip will make all the spokes provided you do not break any.

I then laid out the design of the wheel, its spoke angles and rim, so I could lay the wheel right on top of it and set the spokes properly .The first spoke was 1 $\frac{3}{4}$ inches long going clear across from side to side, with one rim under and the other rim laid on top of it. A hole just snug for a lill, or small $\frac{1}{2}$-inch bank pin, was then bored through rim, spoke and rim, with a very light reaming out with a larger drill to let the pin head set down snug on the face side of the wheel and to hold better when you cut off and rivet the pin point on the reverse side. Now set the half spoke that sets at right angles to this one. File a slight notch in the middle of the spoke just put in and cut the end of the half spoke to fit it and rivet it in place to the rims. Set the opposite half spoke the same way. We only are concerned just now with the fastening of each spoke at the rims, getting them set true to the angles as laid out, one going in between each of the spokes we have just set at right angles, or a spoke at every 45 degrees. The reach of 21 inches from tip to tip is reduced by the converging of the spokes to less than seventeen inches at the rim. Fit the spokes snug and tight together where they butt at the hub, and when all are riveted to the rims, set the two hub discs, one under and one over the hub, being very careful to set them exactly central and so to hold them both by boring a pin hole in the center and driving in a pin to keep them from slipping when you bore a pin hole near the rim of the hub piece and put a pin through each spoke. Be careful to see that you have the face side of the wheel up, so the heads of the pins will all show on the same side. Cut off and rivet all these pin ends at the hub and then your steering wheel begins to look like the real thing.

If the wheel were a little larger we might put a fancy star-headed pin at one spoke, the king spoke, by feeling which a man can tell on a dark night when he has the helm amidships or how many spokes off center it takes to steer her when sailing close-hauled. Another even more popular way was to turn one spoke, the king spoke, with a series of rings or grooves about the hand-grip so it could be identified by the feel of it. The tiller ropes were always rove around the barrel, or drum, as some call it, so this king spoke was uppermost when the helm was dead amidships.

I find I am using the old sea phraseology. A sailor never says another ship is directly abaft his own ship. She is "dead aft," or if forward, she is "dead ahead," or dead abeam, dead amidships, etc. The term is never applied to any intermediate bearing, three points off the starboard bow or two points abaft the beam, etc., but only to signify being in an exact line forward, aft, or amidships. Neither is it used to signify positions above or below.

If one has a small lathe the spokes can be turned out of boxwood with microscopic accuracy and show a beautifully shaped set of spokes; if not, the spokes can be shaped with a file by spinning the spoke between the fingers. At the hub and the rim the spoke is left square.

To complete the wheel take a thin piece of wood. I used mahogany, but it is a matter of personal like or dislike what kind of wood you use. Some like the wheel all of the same colored wood, others like the contrast between the white ash or boxwood spokes and a mahogany or black walnut rim. Very little of it shows anyway for you cut small segments of a circle just enough wider than the two brass rim pieces to make a protruding half-round edge on both inside and outside. Make a snug, tight fit and as each segment is jammed into its place between the rims from spoke to spoke and held by a pin rivet, you will be surprised how strong that wheel becomes. The main thing is to make true, square-edged joints of the rim segments so as not to warp the wheel out of a true plane. Bore out and with a square rat-tailed file make a square hole through the hub to take the end of the steering drum shaft.

I began my wheel as an experiment to see if I could build up such a wheel, "shipshape and Bristol fashion," as anything done in a smart and seaman-like manner was characterized by sailors in the days of sail. I did not stop to shape each spoke before I put it in, but when the whole thing was riveted together I became so enthusiastic over it that I took a small file and shaped each spoke and handgrip afterwards. It was in working on it this way that I realized how rigid the previously flimsy little wheel had become when all the segments of the rim had been jammed in and riveted into place.

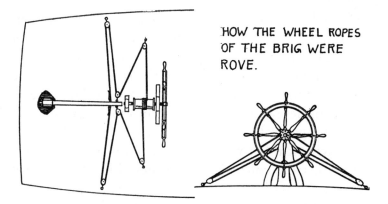

HOW THE WHEEL ROPES
OF THE BRIG WERE
ROVE.

Removing the long hand tiller I stowed it in cleats under the bulwark, aft, on the port side, for use in an emergency, and made a shorter one only 4 feet 6 inches long, from the forward side of the rudderhead, and put two eyebolts in each side close to the forward end. A wooden barrel or drum was fastened to a hard brass shaft by a pin put through both. The after end of this shaft was turned down (filed down) a little in its diameter to fit into a vertical stanchion set into the deck just forward of the tiller's end. Two feet forward of this, the shaft and the wheel were supported by an inverted V bracket that held the shaft horizontal 2 feet 6 inches above the deck, the wheel setting about 6 inches forward of this bracket, with the binnacle just in front of it.

The tiller rope was made fast to the after eye in the tiller and then rove through a single block hooked into

an eyebolt abreast of it, out in the waterways, then back
through a single block hooked into the forward eye in
the tiller, then out through another single block, opposite the middle of the drum, hooked into an eyebolt in
the deck, two feet in from the rail, and then in around
the drum (8 inches in diameter and 18 inches long)

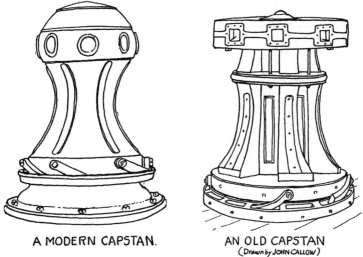

A MODERN CAPSTAN.   AN OLD CAPSTAN
                          (Drawn by JOHN CALLOW)

nine turns and then similarily rove off on the other side.
It takes three revolutions of this wheel to put the helm
hard up or hard down from dead center, or six turns
from hard-a-port to hard-a-starboard, and there is pur-
chase enough so a helmsman would not get thrown
over the wheel when she bucks badly. This wheel added
wonderfully to the shippy look of the brig and was well
worth the work it took to make it.

The capstan is another most important fitting on a
ship. By means of it the anchors were raised in the days
when hemp cables were used, and in olden times, when
both main and foreyards were often lowered down,
they were hoisted by means of the jeer tackles, the haul-

ing ends of which were taken around capstans abaft each mast. On large men-of-war these capstans were generally down on the main deck below the light upper deck. With a fiddler atop the big, flat, capstan head, and some half a hundred men breasted up against the long capstan bars, it was "stamp and go" to wind those

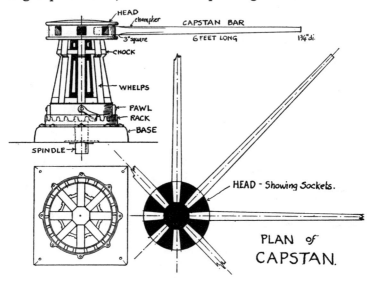

big, heavy yards on a battleship up to the mast bounds. The capstan's spindle went up through two or three decks with two capstans, one on each deck, so men could man the bars on two decks at one and the same time or, as in later years on the big line-of-battle ships, one capstan could be uncoupled and each worked independently.

The capstan on our brig is placed between the second and third deck beam, abaft the after hatchway, and is 2 feet in diameter across the head and stands 3 feet above the deck, 4 inches of which is an oak pad reënforcement above the planking of the deck, the pad being 30 inches square. The head is made of two copper discs, the size, but not so thick, of a copper penny, set so their outer surfaces are six inches apart, leaving room between them for a 3-inch square capstan bar. All the old wooden capstans had square bar holes, "pigeon holes," as sailors called them, tapered as they went back into the capstan head so the bar set in snug and firm. There are eight of these bar holes or sockets in our brig's capstan head and they are the hardest part of the whole capstan to make. You cannot make a satisfactory job out of one piece of wood, with all the sockets cut into it, as the cross grain will soon snap in two, but you can use hard rubber or fibre. The best way is to lay out the arrowhead-shaped segments between the center lines of each bar and cut out such pieces like pieces cut out of a pie and when all are fitted together, a rivet through each piece and through the top and bottom metal discs will hold all together, with no cross grain to split. You can thus get a clean cut, square, socket hole for each bar far better than by boring a round hole and trying to work it out square with a file.

With the head of the capstan finished we now make the barrel. The spindle, the center part or core of the capstan should be 3 feet by the scale of ⅜-inch to the foot or 1⅛ actual inches long. The upper ⅝ of an inch of this, shape octagonally ¼ inch thick, and from there down, round, slightly smaller in diameter. On each of the eight faces of the octagonal part glue and pin fasten the "whelps," as they are called, around which the rope is wound. These are a stout 1⁄16-inch in width and are shaped as shown. Under these fit a ⅛-inch thick disc of wood, a hole in its center permitting it to slide up snug against the lower ends of the whelps. On this disc we have to pivot several metal pawls that drop down and engage against a saw-tooth circular rack of metal fastened down to the ⅛-inch thick deck pad, so the capstan will hold itself from spinning back when the men have a heavy strain on it. Let the spindle extend through the deck pad just far enough to put a metal washer and a toggle pin to keep the capstan from coming loose; then by nailing down the four corners of the deck pad into deck beams we can secure the capstan in place. The spindle should really extend down to the deck below and house into a socket between the lower deck beams. In this instance I have departed from the usual practice of giving the sizes on the ⅜-inch scale and given them in actual inches.

The pawls and pawl rack require a bit of metal work. The pawls, ¼-inch in length, can be filed out to shape and drilled for a pin on which they work, but the rack is a bit more difficult to make. I took a strip of 1/16-inch square brass and filed one side like a saw or rack. Then I bent this around a disc of wood, and around the outer edge I bent a thin strip of brass so it made a fence-like edge around the outer edges of the rack's teeth, so with the block of wood inside and this belt or raised edge outside, a groove was formed around in which the pawls traveled and dropped successively over the saw teeth or cogs against which they engaged and prevented the capstan from turning but the one way. The outer strip of brass was soldered to the toothed rack and both were bored through and pinned fast to the deck pad of wood through which, of course, the spindle of the capstan passed. It being only a small capstan I used but four pawls. If it had been a larger circumference more pawls might be used. To make the pawls fall readily and engage against the rack it was customary to make them heaviest at the free end.

To unite the metal disc heads to the barrel of the

capstan, I happened to have a short piece ($\frac{5}{8}$ of an inch) of tool-steel about $\frac{3}{32}$ of an inch square. I filed a square hole through the two copper discs in the head, bored a slightly smaller hole in the wooden barrel and drove this steel core in, which united both parts securely. Between the whelps, where the little shoulder comes, small chocks should be fitted to make it a complete circle at that point. As this is pretty small work, I squeezed in some plastic wood and when it had dried hard, shaped it down with a penknife. If the capstan were larger, panels might be fitted back in between the whelps for appearance. If made of boxwood and painted white in the panels between the whelps, a very handsome-looking capstan can be produced, with a white enamel finish on the top of the head. Never paint the face of the whelps as the messenger and other ropes wound around it would soon wear it all off.

Capstan bars or heavers for turning the capstan now have to be made. These are eight in number, of ash, 6 feet in length and 3 inches square at the capstan, tapered square to fit into the socket of the capstan head and turned down to a round, tapering from 4 inches to $1\frac{3}{4}$ inches in diameter at the outer end. Leave them bright, natural wood, unpainted, and to stow them, about the only available place we have on this busy little brig is in racks on the mast, stowing the bars vertically. This capstan is a little smaller than the navy's standard of later years where the bars were 8 feet long and 6 inches square at the capstan head, the whole capstan being a little larger in diameter.

The next item we come to is the afterhatch just forward of the capstan. Going down the ladder in this hatchway lands one in the wardroom, the main living-room for all the officers except the commander, generally a lieutenant in naval rank, who has, as seamen always term it, a holy sanctuary all to himself, away aft in the stern, separated from the common petty officers, to preserve his dignity and authority. This hatch is four feet square, in the clear.

In working the capstan, a grating is fitted into the rabbet cut around on the inside of the hatch coamings and that is how I fitted out our little brig. Not having laid the lower deck flooring there was no ladder in place, but the grating hid all this besides adding greatly to the appearance of the brig's deck. White holly or boxwood strips of wood halved into each other and then set into a frame, while it is careful, tedious work, well repays one for his time when completed. With machinery, where great precision in depth of cut and width of cut and spacing can be made with mechanical accuracy, perfection is attained in making these small gratings as professionally-made models testify. The scores can be cut across a solid piece of wood and then with a fine guage saw, any size slats may be ripped off all uniform in width.

Others get a block of steel, the size of their largest grating, and have some machinist mill this on its upper surface with a series of square-cut slots running one way, cut the depth of the grating slats, and across it, at right angles, another equal distance spaced series of slots cut only half as deep. This leaves a surface of little steel squares that is hardened by tempering the steel. With such a block of prepared steel, the slats are laid in the deep grooves and filed down through the shallow grooves. This prevents the small blocks of wood from breaking off. Two sets of slats are so made and then one set fitted reversed so the grooves engage one into the other and the whole is squeezed accurately together in a wide-jawed vise. A more truly shipshape grating is made if only one set of slats is cut half through and the others crossing them are not notched but only made half as thick, for that is how many real gratings are made.

Then make a frame to fit in the hatchway. A frame is three or four inches wide in the real ship. Notch the ends of the grating slats into the inner edges of this frame. The thin slats go in full depth and the thick ones are notched so only the upper half lets down into the frame. Few small model gratings are so notched into the frame, merely being cut to fit in snug and glued fast. Another way is to use a sheet of $\frac{3}{32}$-inch thick celluloid. Get a light brown color in preference to a snow white, if you can, as it looks more natural and does not stare at you so hard. Lay out your slats on this in pencil, leaving the proper frame around the edge. Then drill out all the openings and file them out to square holes with a small square rat-tail or tapered file. The after hatch can be in one piece but the main and forehatches being larger, the gratings should be made in two sections as they would otherwise be too heavy and unwieldy. In bad weather solid hatch covers take the place of these gratings. Holes for the cables should be framed in the forward corners of the main hatch grating.

Forward of this after hatch are the ship's pumps and the main fife rail around the mainmast, making an interesting group of deck fittings. Where the pumps go through the deck is reënforced underneath by a block of pine fitted between the deck beams. There is a heavy beam just abaft of the mainmast and between it and the next beam aft is where the holes to take the pumps are cut. One foot ($\frac{3}{8}$ of an inch) each side of the center line bore a hole ¼-inch (actual) to receive the pumps. I had some copper tubing, ¼-inch outside diameter and ³⁄₁₆-inch inside, corresponding on the ³⁄₈-inch scale to which the model was built, to a pipe 8

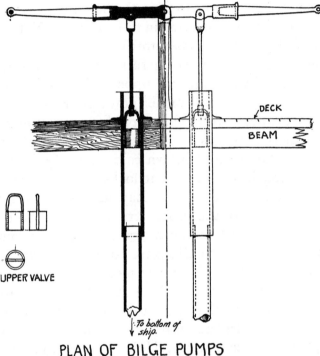

UPPER VALVE

DECK

BEAM

To bottom of ship.

PLAN OF BILGE PUMPS

inches outside and 6 inches inside diameter. This made the valve chamber 4 feet long. Into the lower end of this, about ⅛ of an inch equivalent to 4 inches, I pushed and soldered fast a smaller copper tube that was made long enough to reach down into the bilge between the frames, or floors. The pump chamber stuck up nine inches above the deck with a reamed-out copper washer soldered on there to make a base flange for fastening it to the deck. I did not make a lower valve for the pump although the shoulder where the smaller tube ended in the larger made a good seating for one. But I did simulate an upper valve as they showed when you worked the rocker arms that operated the plungers. I took a short section of the smaller tube and emery-papered it down so it worked freely in the pump chamber. Then I filed a score on each side, outside, and soldered on a short piece of copper wire bent like a stirrup so it gave a bearing to take the lower end of the plunger rod which was flattened out and bent into a loop to go around this stirrup. On the upper end of the plunger rod was soldered a U-shaped piece of flattened-out copper wire which straddled the athwartship rocker arm of the pump and was hinged to it by a pin through a hole bored through all. The plunger rod was made just long enough so the valve came even to the top of the pump chamber at the extremity of the stroke of the rocker arm. The rocker arm was of brass, 2 inches by 1 inch, with an enlarged disc made by a drop of solder on it flattened out and filed where a hole was bored through for the pivot that went through it and the mortice end of the boxwood stanchion set up on end out of the deck into which it was tenoned. This pivot point was three feet above the deck, and the stanchion was 3 inches thick, athwartships, and 6 inches fore and aft. The total length of the rocker arm was 4 feet 2 inches, but 6 inches of this was a socket made of a thin piece of brass folded so it would take the end of a pump heaver 3 inches deep and 1 inch thick and pushed a few inches onto the rocker arm end and soldered fast. I then made a pair of heavers, 2 feet 9 inches long, that just pushed in snug into these sockets. At the outer end I tapered them to a depth of a scant 2 inches leaving a 3-inch circle on the end. Through this circle I bored a hole and soldered in a handlebar that stuck out fifteen inches on each side — the handle about 1¼ inches in diameter.

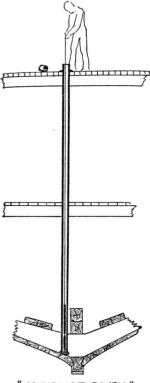

" SOUNDING THE WELL"

As I sat and smoked and looked over my little brig that night, I thought how natural that pumping outfit looked. I pulled the heavers out of their sockets to see where I could find a stowage place for them and then when I laid them on the deck and looked again something was decidedly wrong. Something about that pump jarred on my nerves and I saw right away what it was. That is the worst of being a sketch artist, a bum one, I'll admit, but I realized, right away, I had left off a small detail, unimportant; yes, like a sore thumb. There should be a small reënforcing rim at the edge of the socket where the rocker arms went in, so I took a piece of small copper wire and bent it into a loop that would just ride over the end of the socket and soldered it fast, the solder filleting out the juncture of the two most naturally. Then it did look good. It looked shipshape. But without it the pump was raw and unfinished.

In the space between the same deck beams where the pumps are, the "sounding well" is located. This is a small pipe leading down into the bilge, the same as the pumps do, and being open at the lower end the bilge-water will rise in it as high as it does in the bottom of the ship. To measure how much water there is, a sounding rod is lowered down this pipe and quickly pulled up again to note how far up it is wet. The sounding rod was made in various ways but perhaps the most commonly used type was two, three, or four square rods of iron about ½ inch square and 18 inches in length, flattened at the ends, with holes drilled through so the two adjacent ends could be linked together with wire, so the 6-foot rod could be folded up and stowed more conveniently. This sounding rod was lowered and raised with a light line made fast into the upper eye. Two links might suffice for a small craft while deep-bodied ships would want four links or even more. A screw cap on the top end of this sounding pipe would prevent water on deck from getting below.

The main-bitts and fife rail, built around the mainmast, come next. The main-topsail sheet bitts, which is its full name, consists of two stout vertical timbers, 6 inches square, standing 3 feet 6 inches above the deck and 2 feet 6 inches apart, with a bolster or horizontal piece 6 inches wide and 4 inches thick and 4 feet 6 inches long halved into their forward sides so the top of this bolster comes thirty inches above the deck. On my little brig model these were made of black walnut but should match in color whatever scheme you wish to select; teak, boxwood, or any other hard wood. The bolster piece was held by a large pin driven snug through a bored hole so as not to split the wood and riveted up on each end, or, use the head end on one side and file it down flush with the wood afterwards. The forward edges of these two bitt posts are cut dovetailed with a mortice to receive it, just as was done in the case of the bowsprit bitts, so when the bitt posts were inserted in these holes wedges could be driven in the after ends and the dovetailed forward edges locked securely into the deck and deck frame. A small 3-inch thick knee fitted against the after side, and to the deck,

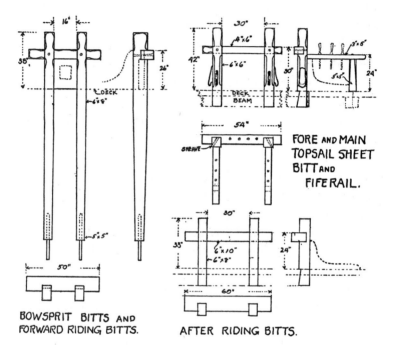

BOWSPRIT BITTS AND
FORWARD RIDING BITTS.

AFTER RIDING BITTS.

FORE AND MAIN
TOPSAIL SHEET
BITT AND
FIFE RAIL.

strengthens the bitt post and covers up most of this wedge. Do not get the arms of this knee too clumsy; 4 inches in depth at mid-length of each arm, is heavy enough. Let the after end extend back 30 inches so it will butt up against the vertical stanchion of the pin-rail, a 3-inch by 5-inch rail that sets on the upper arm of the knee at the bitt post and this 5-inch square stanchion aft of it. Its after edge is three feet from the forward edge of the 6 by 6-inch bitt post.

But there is more to the making of a set of main-bitts than this if we want to make them look realistic, and the little touches that change a crude, square bulk of timber into a shippy-looking set of bitts, are the slight chamfering off of all square corners. You should remember that in a gale of wind men get bowled along or across the deck, by seas breaking aboard, as if they were a set of ninepins; and to fetch up with your ribs or limbs against a sharp corner, is to invite trouble. It is damaging enough even when these sharp corners are killed by chamfering. Leave the work square in the corners and begin the chamfer a couple of inches away from the deck or adjacent piece of work.

At the ends of the bolster and the tops of the bitt posts do more than chamfer. Round the corners slightly so a hitch of a rope thrown around them can be slacked away even when under quite a strain. This is often necessary as when slacking away on a topsail sheet, when the men are clewing up topsails, and the man holding the turn of the topsail sheet about the bitt head has to pay it out as the men tighten up on the clewline; yet not so fast that the sail gets slack enough to slap, for one such slap will often split a topsail from head to foot. A light chamfer will do at the extremities, but close in, where the two pieces of wood cross, increase the chamfer. That is where the heavy strain comes and this also tends to prevent the rope riding out over the ends. The excessive up pull on a topsail sheet requires bitts of this size to stand the pull. A block would not stand it and solid iron sheaves, to prevent their being crushed, are set into a mortice cut diagonally through each bitt post, close down to the deck, so the sheet enters it at the middle of the face of the bitt and comes out just clear of the knee of the outer corner. A cleat is also bolted fast on the outer side of the bitt post to hitch a rope under, coming down from aloft, before it is taken to and belayed on a belaying pin in the pinrail, so the pull is downward on the pinrail.

The main hatch, forehatch, and the foremast bitts and fife rail or pinrail, are a repetition of those already

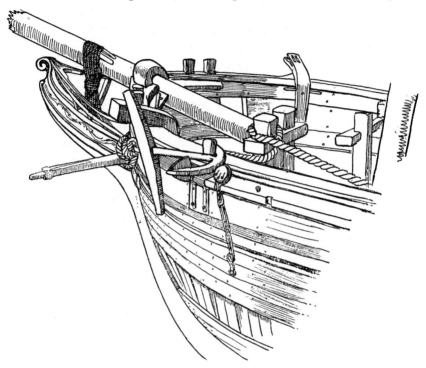

given. We now have to consider the riding or mooring bitts. These come just aft of the foremast fife rail, just aft of and abutting against the heavy pardner beam, to take the heavy strain or pull these bitts are subjected to when the ship is riding to her anchors. The uprights or posts are 6 inches, athwartships, and 8 inches, fore and aft. They are set 2 feet 6 inches apart, face to face, and standing 2 feet 9 inches above the deck. The bolster piece, 6 inches by 10 inches and 5 feet long, is set into the after face of the bitt posts so its upper face is 2 feet above the deck and 9 inches below the top of the posts. Half is taken out of each piece and the after edge of the bolster is rounded and the edges of the heads are chamfered so where the heavy cable goes around them there will be no sharp corners. In fact many capstans had hard wood cheeks fitted to each face of the bitt head and bolster, to round them out where the big 6- and 8-inch diameter hempen cable was wound around the bitts, for being able to veer out cable quickly, when anchored in a crowded roadstead, more than once has been the means of saving a ship from heavy damages and even possible loss. The knees to these bitts extend forward to better resist the pull which is in that direction.

A cable of such size cannot be hitched around a bitt head so it is given an S-shaped twist about the forward bitts and then the end is stoppered with lashings or carried on aft and given another similar twist about the after-riding bitts and the end then stoppered. The starboard cable is brought aft, under the bolster piece of the riding bitts outside the vertical bitt post and then taken inside the bitt head, over the bolster, around forward of it and aft on the outside. The bight is taken around "with the sun," as it is designated from left to right, and then its end is lashed to the deck stoppers, short pieces of stout hemp rope lashed to eyebolts in the deck in line with the cable abaft of the bitt head. The port cable is brought aft on the outside of the bitt also, under the bolster, but the bight is turned around the bitt head the opposite way "against the sun," right to left as you stand facing forward. The stoppers, generally two, are passed around a thimble in a stout eyebolt in the deck secured with a "throat seizing" where it is doubled back across itself and then the two parts are laid to-

gether and a seizing put around both, a "round seizing"
as it is termed. In the end of this 2-foot or so long stopper, a stopper knot (a double wall with ends whipped)
is worked. A lanyard spliced around this stopper, under
the knot, is then wrapped several turns around the cable,
the knot on the end of the stopper preventing their

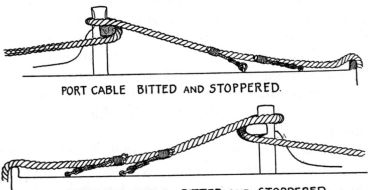

PORT CABLE BITTED AND STOPPERED.

STARBOARD CABLE BITTED AND STOPPERED.

slipping off, when the cable is laid alongside of the
stopper. The cables are passed down the main hatchway and coiled down below amidships. A small hole is
cut out of each forward half of the main hatch grating
to receive the cable.

The cables for such a brig as ours are given in several books of various dates. In the Merchants and Ship-
masters Manual, published in 1864, we find that for a
vessel the size of the *Lexington*, a craft of 166 tons, the
tables in that book give for a 160-ton craft, a $^{15}\!/_{16}$-inch
size chain cable, and that her anchors should be 800-
pounds weight. Another table which includes a hemp
cable gives:— 150-ton ship— 1-inch chain, or $10\frac{3}{4}$-
inch circumference rope and the anchors at 800 pounds.
Another table of comparative strength of chain and
hemp cable, gives $^{15}\!/_{16}$-inch chain, a proof of $12\frac{1}{2}$

tons, and a 10-inch rope, as 22 tons. The weight of a 10-inch cable-laid rope, for 100 fathoms, is 1921 pounds and a 10½-inch one is 2119 pounds. Both are given as the equivalent of a 1-inch chain cable. This shows us that we need 800-pound anchors and about 10-inch circumference hemp cables.

On consulting Lloyd's own book of rules of 1870 we find a 150-ton ship should carry two bower anchors, one stream anchor and one kedge anchor. Exclusive of the stock the bower anchors must each weigh 650 pounds, the stream anchor, 250 pounds, and the kedge, 125 pounds. Only the size of the stream anchor's hawser is given and that is 6 inches circumference. In 1870 it was assumed that nothing but chain would be used on the bowers and they are given as $1\frac{5}{16}$-inch stud link chain and the equivalent of a $1\frac{5}{16}$-inch chain is a $9\frac{1}{2}$-inch circumference rope. A 1-inch chain is equivalent to a 10-inch circumference rope. So we may safely assume our cables to be between $3\frac{1}{4}$ and $3\frac{1}{2}$ inches in diameter.

Another old rule was to allow 500 pounds per hundred tons for vessels smaller than frigates. When we apply this rule we get practically the same result or 830 pounds weight for our anchors.

But even after knowing the weight of the anchor we are still all at sea as to its dimensions. The general rule for proportioning an anchor is to make the flukes as long as the shank, from the crown to the top of the stock. The stock, in length, is equal to the shank, plus one-half the diameter of the ring. The palm is half the length of one fluke, or arm, from shank to bill, as the point of the fluke is termed, and as wide as they are long. The stock is square, in size one inch for every foot of length of the shank.

We can approximate the size of iron of which to make our anchor by calculating how many cubic feet it takes to make up 800 pounds of iron. With a 6-foot shank and a 6-foot fluke piece we have 12 feet and if we take 5-inch square iron we have 2 cubic feet of

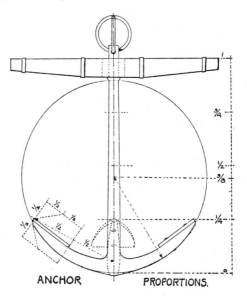

ANCHOR   PROPORTIONS.

metal which, at 450 pounds per cubic foot, gives us a weight of 900 pounds. So we can forge our anchor out of 4½-inch square iron and come very close to our desired weight (4½ inches = .357 ft.: : .375 × .375 × 12 × 450 = 750 pounds). What metal comes off the flukes or arms is made up by the metal in the palms, and the reduction in the top of the shank is made up by the increase in metal at the crown.

We can closely approximate the size our anchors must be, to give the required weight, by an old rule which give us the following:

To find the weight of an anchor in tons—cube the length of the shank and divide by 1160, or inversely,

the length is found—by multiplying the weight by
1160, and the cube root of the product will equal the
length of shank.

The arms equal ⅜ of the shank and form an arc 120
degrees of a circle whose center is ⅜ of the length of
shank.

The flukes equal half the length of the arms, and
their breadth is ⅖ of the arm.

The thickness (circumference) at the throat equals
⅕ of the shank's length.

The thickness at the small end to be ⅔ that at the
throat.

The small ends of the arms, at the flukes, equal ¾
the circumference at throat.

The wood stock is the same length as the shank and
is square, 2½ times the shank in the middle.

So if we make our anchor's shank 8 feet long, we
find by this rule that $8 \times 8 = 64 \times 8 = 5120$ and this
divided by 1160 gives us .44 tons or 880 lbs, which is
about the weight required.

The arms ⅜ of the shank: ⅜ of 8 = 3 feet.

The flukes ½ the arms: ½ of 3 = 1.5 feet.

The width of flukes ⅖ the arms: ⅖ of 3 = 1.2 feet.

The thickness at throat ⅕ the shank: ⅕ of 8 = 1.6
feet circumference.

The thickness at small end ⅔ that at throat: ⅔ of
1.6 = 1.05 feet circumference.

The stock to be 2½ times as thick as the shank in
the middle. The mean of the shank's diameter at throat
and end is 1.3 circumference, about 5½ inches in di-
ameter and $2\frac{1}{2} \times 5\frac{1}{2} = 13.75$ or 13¾ inches square
for the wooden stock at the shank. It tapers on the
under side and sides until it is ⅔ this at the ends or
about 9 inches square.

We thus have a starting point in determining the size and shape of our anchors; and much depends on getting a shippy-looking anchor. If the metal is made too small in diameter or in square, the anchor has a skinny look like the long-fluked sand anchors some southern fish schooners carry; and if made too heavy, it doesn't look at all efficient or as if it had any holding power. It then looks like a steamboat anchor.

You never see a Gloucesterman come in, one of those powerful, seagoing and sea-keeping schooners, but that you hear some real, deepwater sailorman comment on the efficiency of her ground tackle. "Just look at them anchors! Them is anchors that will hold a man till kingdom come," and similar phrases of admiration are heard for the apparent holding power of the long-shanked, broad-palmed, mud hooks, with a long wooden stock, that will insure an anchor's turning over so its flukes can dig in or catch hold on the bottom. They are the result of years of experience in anchoring on the ledges of the Grand Banks. Deepwater ship's anchors have somewhat this same feature except with a noticeable increase in heft of metal that gives them a more ponderous and substantial look.

The arms or flukes are a radius of ⅜ of the length of the shank from the crown and a line across their tips or bills will cross the shank ¼ of its length up from the crown. But it is the shape the various parts are forged out to, that makes the appearance of an anchor. The shank is square in section with edges slightly chamfered and tapered at the stock to ⅔ of what it is at the crown. The flukes are bent on a radius equal to ⅜ the length of the shank, from crown to top of stock, and this shape is held on the upper edge, but the lower edge is to be filed down so it comes to a blunt point at the

outer end or bill and only regains its full depth half
way out and is slabbed or tapered off on the sides, be-

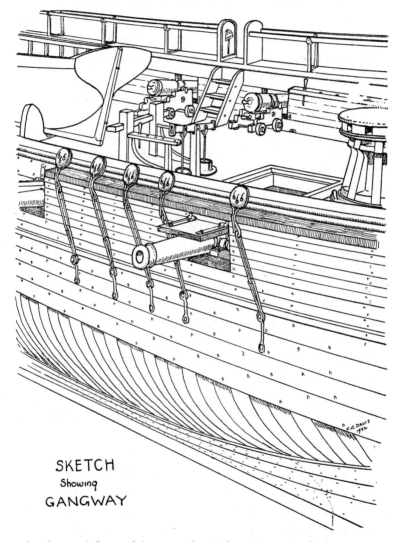

SKETCH
Showing
GANGWAY

ginning with nothing at the inboard end of the palm,
to one-third its width at the bill. At the crown, the
juncture of the shank and the flukes, the corners are to

be well filleted out with solder, to give strength at this important point.

With a few timberheads put down through the rail and their tops neatly chamfered off on the corners, the woodwork on our hull is nearly completed. Two of these, forming a bow chock for head lines, go just forward of the bow-chaser port. A single one, just forward of the first side port, provides a substantial lashing place for the anchor when we want to stow it, with the ring lashed to the cathead, and the inner fluke around this timberhead so the shank comes up against it and can be lashed fast, with stock standing vertical and flukes horizontally resting on the rail. Aft, there are two more timberheads for stern lines. These were 6 inches square and stuck up 9 inches above the rail.

Had she been a larger vessel, such as a sloop-of-war of 20 guns or even a small-sized frigate, we might have fitted her out with a "horse block" at her gangway, but being only a small brig-of-war, a short gangway ladder of three steps was made and hooked to eyebolts inside her bulwarks between the two gun ports just forward of her main channels. The "horse block" is a small grating platform, about 3 feet square, that hooks onto the rail so it lays flush with it and is supported on a couple of iron stanchions set into deck sockets, with a ladder from it to the deck. Its name may sound queer to this generation, where the sight of a horse is unusual, but in my childhood days many an hour I played on the horse block at my Aunt Taylor's cottage in Rochdale, New York. It was a platform, about 4 feet square, built on the top rail of the fence, with steps leading up to it from the front yard. Nearly every cottage down that one and only street that ended at Taylor's mill at the creek, had its horse block. Carriages drove up alongside the fence, for there were no stone or brick sidewalks, only a dirt path, and their occupants could step out onto the horse block and go down four or five steps into the yard; yet roving cows, mules, or horses were kept out. So you see the term "horse block" had a special significance to old people. Here, on a ship, the commanding officer used to take his station when the evolution of tacking ship was to be enacted and roar out his orders through his speaking trumpet. It was a sort of sacred precinct reserved for the use of officers and guests. The common jack-tars could climb over the hammock nettings and get into their boats by way of a Jacob's ladder hanging down under the swinging or boat-boom from the fore channels, on the port side. I made my side ladder out of white ash, 2 inches thick, putting three treads or steps into grooves cut with a panel saw and the two side pieces were held firmly 3 feet apart, the width of the treads, by wires under each step riveted on the outside of the 9-inch wide side pieces.

The hammock berthing or hammock nettings built up on top of the rail, change the appearance of the brig's deck considerably and add a strong touch of realism to her man-of-war appearance which only needs the longboat stowed amidships and the guns and gun carriages, with their accoutrements, to complete.

The rail was about on a level with a man's elbow, 3 feet 2 inches above the deck, but with the hammock rail rigged up, only his head showed, and when the hammocks were stowed and hammock cloths laced over them, only the top of a man's head would show above it. The hammock rails, set in metal brackets that fastened to the top of the rail, measured 4 feet 9 inches

to the deck and it was about 5 feet 6 inches to the top
of the stowed hammocks. It is this high bulwark that
stamps a vessel as a man-of-war perhaps more than any
other feature. The hammocks served as sandbags to an
army's embankment, to stop small shot.

The trough-like box, in which the hammocks were
stowed on a small man-of-war, was built sometimes en-

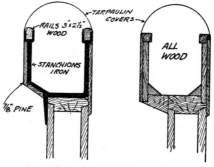

HAMMOCK NETTINGS.

tirely of wood and sometimes in a combination of metal
brackets and wooden sides and bottom, the rail itself
forming the bottom. On large vessels and old ships-of-
war, where, in the waist, there were no bulwarks so as
to make it easier to hoist out the ship's boats, the hammock nettings were rail high and supported on removable iron stanchions. Netting, supported by the two
parallel rails at the top of the stanchions, hung down
like a bag or trough about 14 inches wide and in these
the hammocks, each with its bedding or blankets rolled
up into a compact wad and lashed so, were stowed away
in the daytime. Hammock clothes painted black were
laced outside and in, with a flap over the top that
formed the lid to this hammock stowage place. It gives
a clumsy, heavy appearance to a ship's rail and yet on
a war vessel is most appropriate. Just as the huge,

clumsy wooden davits on a whaler are a distinct emblem of her trade, so are the clumsy hammock rails to
a man-of-war. Start the hammock boxes abreast of the
middle shroud in the fore rigging and let it run aft to
the gangway where, 2 feet apart, are set up the billboards, the front door, so to speak, of the ship. The
face side of these billboards were most elaborately
carved with national emblems, the American eagle,
flags, floral designs, or the liberty cap at the top of a
flagpole, a favorite emblem in the days of the Revolution. They stood up 2 feet 8 inches above the rail.
From the gangways these hammock boxes or nettings
ran aft to a point opposite the end of the tiller.

The wooden box hammock stowage was more popular in times of peace but was not so desirable a fitting
in war time on account of the flying splinters of wood
that would be sent spinning through the air by an
enemy's shot in a real battle at sea. So we have fitted
out our little brig with metal brackets, wooden rails,
and hammock nettings with tarpaulin covers.

The small boats carried by a brig-of-war like the
Lexington, would be a longboat stowed in chocks on
the main deck between the masts; a first cutter hanging on the starboard davits well aft; a second cutter
hanging on the port davits opposite; and a gig hanging
at the stern davits. Their size is determined by the rule
of the Navy, as follows: To find the length of the first
launch, multiply the square root of the length of the
ship by 2.6; the breadth is $\frac{1}{4}$ the length so found. The
first and second cutters of ships-of-the-line and the first
cutters of sloops-of-war to be .9 of the launch. The
third and fourth cutters of ships-of-the-line, and second cutters of sloops-of-war to be .9 the first cutter.
Quarter, waist, or stern boats to be the same dimensions

as the third and fourth cutters of ships-of-the-line, or second cutters of sloops-of-war, only built lighter. Gigs are the same dimensions as third and fourth cutters.

The proportional length of boat's oars, outboard; for double-banked boats, 1.25 of beam of launch, 1.30 for first cutter, 1.40 for second cutter, 1.45 for third cutter. For single-banked boats, their beam multiplied by 2.20 for fourth cutter and whaleboats; for gigs, multiply by 2.5.

A little brig like ours would not carry a launch. Her largest boat, the longboat, would be equivalent to a first cutter. So to find its size we find the square root of 90 feet which is about 9.5 feet (as 9.5 × 9.5 = 90.25 and our brig is 90 feet). 9.5 multiplied by .9 equals 24.7 feet, the launch size, but we carry none so we find .9 of 24.7 feet for the length of the next smaller-sized boat, the first cutter of a ship-of-the-line, or, as in our case, the longboat, and we get a length of 22.25 feet and ¼ of this or 5½ feet is her beam.

The quarter boats are .9 of the longboat or 20 feet by 5 feet beam; and the boat on the stern davits is the same length and beam. The size of a small boat's keel is found by multiplying its breadth of beam by .4, which gives the size in inches. The siding of the frames is .5 of the keel; the moulded depth of frames at heel is 1.5 of the siding, and at the head .5 of the heel. The thickness of the planking is the boat's breadth in feet multiplied by .10.

But the shape of the small boats is important. There is a distinct difference in the look of the small boats on deep-water ships from the sharp-ended, lean-bodied boats used along shore in protected waters. Merchant ships, in particular, have a bulky appearance to their boat's form that seems to resemble somewhat the burdensomeness of the ship herself. They are made to carry a big load. The famous Whitehall boats we used to see moored in the boat slip at the Battery, in New York, were used by the Battery boatmen to row captains and shipping men off to the ships that used to be anchored in a fleet down off Bedloe's Island, when the statue of Liberty was being erected, and by the Hell Gate pilots at City Island, who rowed out and boarded ships coming down Long Island Sound. They were a product of such master boat builders as old A. B. Wood and a few other South Street boat builders who perfected this clean-lined, easily-rowed, lap-strake type of boat. Men like Moriarity and Glove specialized in the carvel-built, more bulky ship's boat. Men-of-war boats were all built at the Navy Yards, from standard designs or moulds whose shape had been proven by experience.

The smallest cutters on the second class line-of-battle-ship *North Carolina*, were of the following dimensions: 30 feet long, 7 feet 6 inches beam, and 2 feet 7 inches in depth. The next largest size was 33 feet, by 8 feet 5 inches, by 3 feet 2 inches, and the largest cutters were 36 feet, by 9 feet 6 inches, by 3 feet 6 inches. While these figures give us a slight variation in proportion of beam to length, such as .4, 3.9, and 3.8, in the case of the relative depth to beam they are all a ratio of 2.7; that is, the beam is 2.7 times the depth, or the beam divided by 2.7 equals the required depth. By this rule our 22-foot boat, of 5½ feet beam, would be 2.44 feet in depth. And our 20-foot boat, of 5 feet beam, would be 2.22 feet in depth.

All navy boats, except perhaps the admiral's barge or captain's gig, were very full, bluff-bowed boats at the gunwale, however much fined away below. They generally were rowed with thole pins. Some of the big ones, however, had a wash strake above the gunwale and had what were termed wash-strake rowlocks, square cutouts, metal lined, in which the oars worked.

In a large volume issued by the Navy Department, in 1844, entitled "Tables of Allowances of Equipment, Outfits, Stores, &c., &c., &c., for each class of vessels in

PLAN OF THE CUTTERS.

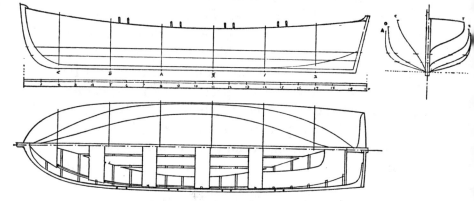

the Navy of the United States" in the carpenter's department we find the boats allowed for brigs-of-war as follows: —

Launch, 24 feet long, 6 feet 10 inches beam, 3 feet depth.

First cutter, 22 feet long, 6 feet beam, 2 feet 6 inches depth.

Second cutter, 22 feet long, 5 feet 6 inches beam, 2 feet 2 inches depth.

Third cutter, 22 feet long, 5 feet 6 inches beam, 2 feet 2 inches depth.

These boats are all slightly larger than we have before calculated that we needed for the *Lexington,* but the reason is that the brigs of 1840 were a hundred feet or more in length, with a 72 foot mainmast, 64 foot 8 inch foremast, and 59 feet 6 inch main yard, larger vessels than our brig *Lexington*.

I had gone ahead and made a longboat for my brig, whittling it out by eye to see how such a boat would look when stowed in chocks, amidships, to have one shown in the photograph. This is the one whose lines are here shown. She measures 22 feet in length, 5 feet in beam, and 3 feet 1 inch in depth. So she is 6 inches narrower and 9 inches deeper than the Navy's proportions. But she looks so well in her chocks on deck I shall leave her there. I hollowed her out inside with a gouge one night, undercutting the gunwale inside with an old lance so that when I bent the frames in they would jam fast and stay in place. When I held her up in the sunlight, the next day, I was surprised to see I had her so thin the sunlight shone through her sides. After all her frames were bent in you could see each one by holding her up to the light.

The frames were made of ¹⁄₁₆-inch strips of thick cardboard, not too hard, painted with orange shellac, and the inside of the boat was treated to the same, as each frame went in, which firmly stuck them in place as it hardened. A thin, wooden strip was then bent in, fore and aft, on each side, 10 inches below the gunwale, as a seat riser, and on this the thwarts all rested. A few tiny pin points and wet shellac held this riser in place and they helped to hold the frames. The seats were then put in as shown on the plan. A few floors were put across in the bottom and on them the floor boards were laid. She was all finished in orange shellac, with rudder and tiller and oars 12 feet long, to row 4 oars, single banked. The top strake and gunwale were painted black.

The cutters, being davit boats and having to clear the after gun, are all the better for not being so deep,

so in their case I first drew a design to the regulation
dimensions and then made my boats from templates

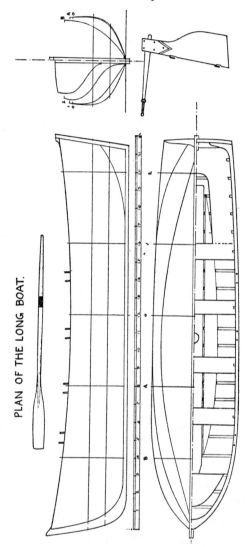

PLAN OF THE LONG BOAT.

shaped to this design. Most large craft and even some
of the little brigs, carried whaleboat-shaped cutters on
their quarter davits, being swung out ready to lower

away quickly in case a man fell overboard. The whale-boat model was considered a better-shaped boat to handle under rough water conditions. However, the square-sterned cutters carry more and are better to transfer boarding parties. We carry the whaleboat on the stern davits for emergencies.

Cut these davits with a slight curve on the outboard end and fasten them to the outside of the bulwarks through a framehead. In the outer end cut two vertical mortices and put in two little brass sheaves in each davit. Let the brass wire that pivots them extend through far enough to turn an eye in each end. The quarter boats will clear the stern davit boat and also the aftermost gun, as there is just length enough between them for a twenty-foot cutter to lower away clear of everything. These davits, like the stern davits, were made out of black walnut, 8 inches square at the rail and tapered to 6 inches square at the head. They stand up 8 feet 6 inches above the rail, being bolted outside the bulwarks through the timberheads; they have an outboard reach at the head of 4 feet 6 inches where two small brass sheaves are inserted in scores cut out to receive them, the same as in the stern davits, with eyes at the sides, the same way to which the span and davit guys may be attached.

In later years, as iron davits came into vogue, they were substituted for the clumsier-looking old balk of timber that was required to make a wooden davit strong enough to carry a boat. They gave a much smarter look to a man-of-war whose men and officers were extremely jealous of their craft's appearance. When the new style, circular skylights were first made by an enterprising Boston firm, the officers on some of the American sloops-of-war clubbed together and contributed enough money out of their personal allowances to buy one for their ship, as the navy regulations would not allow such extravagance, because they wanted to have their vessel as natty looking as some other craft that had procured a circular skylight while being overhauled at Boston. There was the same kind of rivalry for fancy

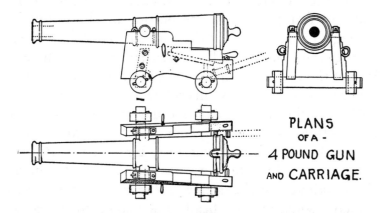

PLANS
OF A -
4 POUND GUN
AND CARRIAGE.

binnacle heads when the tapered, octagonal-shaped, glass-paneled ones were first introduced on light, turned pedestals. But our little brig was of the days before such finery and we must not mix the styles of 1776 with those of 1840.

On frigates and ship-of-the-line that carried boats double-banked on the quarter davits, these members were huge timbers set into sockets at the ship's side. They were straight timbers that stuck out about forty-five degrees from the ship's side and were supported at their outer ends by rope spans that went up to the mizzenmast head. One boat hung at the end and another half way out on the davit.

Last but not the least of all the deck fittings are the cannon. With their gun carriages they are really a formidable job. The cannon require a metal turning lathe and careful workmanship to preserve the character of the muzzle and breech mouldings, reënforcing rings, and the cascable. I furnished a drawing and had a man who specializes in this work turn out my sixteen guns with vent ogee and trunnions all fitted on. The gun carriages, however, I made of black walnut, with wheels made by sawing off sections of a round, black, hard rubber knitting needle, and boring a hole for the axle.

Just as the size of the gun ports, as previously described, were determined by the diameter of the cannon ball, so, also, was the size of the various parts of a gun carriage obtained. The rule was that the thickness of the sides or brackets of the gun carriage should be the same as the diameter of the shot or cannon ball (which, in the case of a four-pound shot, is 3.053 inches) and the axletrees to be the same size but square. The bolts holding this carriage together should be $\frac{1}{5}$ the diameter of the shot.

In a book called "Ordnance Instructions of the United States Navy," published by the Government in 1866, a most complete description of the parts that go to make up a complete gun carriage are most lucidly given. A drawing having reference letters and numbers enables a person to identify the names of all parts and is here reproduced. It shows how the brackets are set parallel to the taper of the gun so the front wheels or "trucks," as they term them, are closer together than the rear trucks, and shows many parts that many never knew or heard of before. Guns are generally "hung by the middle," as it is termed when the trunnion is in the middle of the gun barrel, but back in Revolutionary times, old records show there was some confusion because some guns were "hung by the thirds," that is, the trunnion was ⅓ of the diameter of the gun barrel up from the lower side. When Commodore Macdonough was fitting out the 74-gun ship-of-the-line *Washington*, at Portsmouth, New Hampshire, in 1815, he wrote to the Navy Department asking whether the guns intended for the ship were to be hung by the middle or by the thirds, in order to know how high to make the gun carriages. The gun should center in the gun port so it can equally be elevated or depressed at the muzzle.

On September 16, 1815, Commodore Macdonough wrote to J. Rogers as follows:—

"The 32 pd. guns intended for the lower gun deck have been for some time in the yard. I presume the commissioners were not aware of this and it remains for their order whether these guns or those which are landed from the *Independence* be wanted. These guns are *hung by the third* and the carriages completed agreeable to their dimensions.

"The wood and ironwork for the upper (or second) gun deck carriages are ready for putting together and the carriages are calculated for *center hung* guns, 32 pdrs. The carriages for twenty-six 32 pdrs. carronades are ready for the guns which are in the yard," etc., etc. It may be this was the cause of the dispute in that oft-told anecdote about John Paul Jones and Major Hackett, over gun carriages when fitting out the *Ranger*.

The bolts used in constructing our brig's gun carriages would, according to rule, be ⅝-inches in diameter or about the size of an ordinary pin. The brackets and axletrees, a scant ⅛-inch in actual size. Make a pattern of the shape of the bracket and get all exactly alike before you begin assembling them and the job will be accomplished easier and quicker than if made one at a time.

The following will give you the correct naval terms to apply to each part of the gun carriages.

Nomenclature
of Ordinary Naval Truck-Carriage

Wooden Parts

A. Brackets of large truck-carriages are made each of two pieces joined by a jog "a," and dowelled. The remaining parts of the brackets are the trunnion holes "b," steps "c," quarter rounds "d" and arch "e."

B. Transom let into brackets.

C. Breast piece, in two parts—the inner part fixed, by two bolts into transom; the outer part movable, connected by hinges.

D. Front and rear axletrees, consisting each of square body "f," and arms "g," jogged into brackets.

E. Front and rear trucks.

F. Dumb trucks.

G. Bed and stool.

H. Quoin.

Implements

I. Handspikes.

K. Chocking quoin.

Metal Parts

1. Two cap squares.
2. Four cap-square bolts and two keys and chains.
3. Two bracket bolts.
4. Two rear axletree bolts.
5. Two side tackle eyebolts.

6. One train tackle eyebolt.
7. One transporting eyebolt.
8. Two breast bolts.
9. Two hinges of breast pieces.
10. Two transom bolts (upper and lower).
11. Two breeching side shackles and pins.
12. Bed bolt.
13. Four axletree bands.
14. Chafing plates of steps and brackets.
15. Four linchpins and washers.
16. Quoin plate and stop.
17. Ratchet for quoin stop.
18. Four training loops.
19. Breeching thimble (cast-iron).
20. Side shackle bolts for breechings.
21. Shackle pin, plates, and keys.
22. Two axlestays.
23. Handspike shoe.

Being of a later date than our brig there are several modern improvements on this naval truck carriage such as the side shackle for the breeching, instead of a large eye, and the cascable of the gun as shown has a removable clevice piece held by a pin, for holding the breeching, whereas in our case the breeching rove through the side eyes and clinched at the cascable with a seizing. The same is true with the breeching thimbles at the side of the gun ports. Our brig had only eyebolts.

It requires quite a bit of small detail work to set one of these cannon in its place. First, there are the large eyes for the breechings, one each side of each gun port, through the timberhead that makes the side of the porthole. Then the side tackles require ringbolts fairly well spread away from the port, about 3 feet, so the breech of the gun may be slewed by them and the aid of hand spikes, either forward or aft, according to how the object they are shooting at bears from their ship. Inboard, directly in line with the gun, is a ring-

NAVAL TRUCK CARRIAGE.

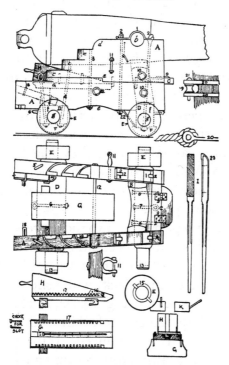

bolt in the deck, into which the train-tackle block, the block and fall by which the gun is run in for reloading, is hooked. Each gun has to have this set of eyebolts and ringbolts and all the breechings, hemp, three-strand, shroud-laid rope and the gun-tackle falls to be a good quality of manila, at least $2\frac{1}{4}$ inches in circumference, rove through 8-inch lignum-vitae sheaved blocks, with hooks no less than $1\frac{1}{4}$ inches in diameter at the bend.

The muzzle of the gun should be at least a foot inside of the bulwarks when run in to permit the charge of powder and then the cannon ball being inserted into the muzzle when loading.

The bow and stern ports will also require all this paraphernalia fitted so that in an emergency a gun could be shifted to fire through them. Because of the extra rake of the ship's side at the ends, which prevents the gun carriage from being run snug up against the bulwarks and so prevents the muzzle from projecting a safe distance outside these ports, we see, in looking over the armament generally carried by these small vessels, along with a broadside of carronades or four-, six- or nine-pound carriage guns, they nearly always had two, long six-pounders or nine-pounders, or whatever it might be, and these were included for just such use as at bow or stern ports.

Over each gun port were two more eyebolts put there so in bad weather the ports could be closed and the gun muzzle butted against the bulwarks and lashed. A gun coming loose on a ship's deck, when she is being tossed about in a heavy sea during a gale, is about the most dangerous mishap that can befall her. That is one argument for a decidedly pronounced swelling at the muzzle, as it holds a lashing from coming adrift.

There are also some little fittings such as rammers and sponges and ladles, the latter for removing shot from a gun, all of which, if provided, add to a model's attractiveness. The finest example of this I have ever seen is a model of a little revenue brig-of-war named the *Washington*, that is stuck away in an out of the way alcove upstairs in the Larchmont Yacht Club at Larchmont, New York, protected under a large glass case. Its value to me is not only its completeness, down to a

deck swab, but the realism portrayed. Whoever made
it performed a labor of love in the making and put into
it individualism. One feels as if he were looking at a
real, honest-to-goodness ship herself. Everything along
her littered-up deck has a use and is made so it looks
in shape and coloring like the object itself. This model
was made by someone whose eyes were familiar with
every item he turned out in such perfection in miniature. He had seen and he had handled all that gear
till it became part of his very life and it is such models
that attract a sailor's attention and take him back to sea
again. They are not shoe-polished, glazed specimens
of furniture-polished woodwork, but real deep-water
ships only reduced in size.

Rammer heads, $\frac{1}{4}$ of an inch less in diameter than
the bore of the gun, were made of well-seasoned ash,
birch, beech, or other tough wood. The face of the
rammer is hollowed so as to embrace the face of the
ball and press the selvagee wad home into its place.
A hole is bored, of $1\frac{1}{2}$ inch diameter, lengthwise
through the head, to admit the tenon turned down on
the end of the $1\frac{3}{4}$-inch diameter staff made of tough
ash. A wooden (hard wood) pin $\frac{3}{10}$ of an inch diameter is driven through both head and tenon of staff.

The rammer staffs are made 1 foot longer than the
bore of the gun. They have grooves $\frac{1}{16}$ of an inch deep
and $\frac{1}{4}$ of an inch wide cut in them to show when the
"ordinary charges" are in place, and, by due allowances, the others also.

Sponge heads are made of poplar, or other suitable
light wood. A hole $1\frac{1}{2}$ inches in diameter is bored
through it, the same as with the rammer, to take the
staff, into which the worm is previously secured by
means of a brass pin which passes through an eye in its

shank and the tenon. The worm is intended to project half an inch beyond the face of the sponge head, when the tenon is in place, and to have free play back into its socket when pressed against the bottom of the bore. It must be 2 inches in length and $1\frac{1}{4}$ inches in diameter, made of elastic brass or composition wire $\frac{2}{10}$ of an inch in diameter, and tapered at the points, so as to preserve its elasticity and firmness. It is to be left-handed, in order to act when turned to the right, or with the sun. The wood of which sponge heads are made should be well seasoned, and got out of a size but little greater than the diameter of the heads for which they are intended, so that there may be as little shrinkage as possible in the finished heads.

The heads, when finished, should also be primed with several coats of boiled linseed oil or varnish, as the porous wood of which they are made is apt to become water-soaked, or to split on exposure to air. When covered with wool, the whole surface should be covered and so sheared as to have no windage, and to be even with the points of the worm, that they may take effect. The head of woolen sponges should be 1 inch less in diameter than the bore of the gun. Sheepskin was abolished in the navy about 1866, but covers for sponge heads, made up to slip over the head and be tacked on, were supplied instead. The heads for sponges were 8 inches long, and all sponge heads intended to be covered with woolen material must be slightly tapered and secured by a thin copper hoop, fastened with copper tacks, on the inner end. Sponge caps to protect them were made of canvas duck, with a becket on the end to facilitate their removal.

Handspikes were 5 feet long, 1.6 inches round at the small end, continuing round for 34 inches, then becoming octagonal for 6 inches and then 2½ inches square for 20 inches. Eighteen inches of the end was metal shod, the radius of the quarter round being 3½ inches.

The stowage of all these various articles adds to the brig's attractiveness. Sling the rammer and sponge in canvas straps or loops from the bulwark just below the rail, in the space between the guns. One with its head forward and the other aft, so they stow snug, and between the guns, close to the bulwark on deck, put a triangular frame in which pile a pyramid of cannon balls. Get shot of a size that will fit the bore of your cannon.

In sparring such a vessel as our brig, we have numerous rules to go by and the question is which rule gives us the spar system in use in the days in which the vessel was rigged. I have given several of these rules in my previous books, the "Ship Model Builders Assistant" and "Ships of the Past," and by a curious coincidence have determined the proper rule. I gave the plans of the U. S. frigate *Raleigh*, which the British Admiralty were kind enough to let me have, as I could find no trace of this Revolutionary craft during extensive research in America. Having captured this ship, they put her in drydock at Portsmouth, England, and on October 21, 1779, measured her and drew up a full plan of her hull. But there was no sail plan so I took the rule I had been studying and, by comparing it with such few authentic sail plans as I had procured, found it to be very accurate, and, using this rule, I drew up a spar plan for the *Raleigh*, which was published in "Ships of the Past."

A year or so later a man out West communicated with me and asked me where I got the sail plan from.

I wrote and told him all the circumstances and in return he sent me a copy of Captain Thompson's original and complete return of the *Raleigh*, with the dimensions of all her spars, boats, etc., and on comparing them with the plan I found no differences worth mentioning. The only variation was a few inches in the length of the topsail yardarms. So I felt if the old rule gave me results as close as that, it was for a fact the same rule they used in those days, and by that rule I have reconstructed the *Lexington's* sail plan.

It is the old English system of sparring ships and is based on the length between the stem and sternpost on deck and the beam measured outside the wales, the extreme beam. To find the whole length of the mainmast, add the length and beam and half this sum is the length required; its diameter is $\frac{7}{8}$ of an inch to every 3 feet of length. The foremast is $\frac{8}{9}$ of the mainmast.

We have no mizzenmast in a brig, but for those who might want to figure out the spars for a ship and to keep the rule complete, we give its proportions, viz.: $\frac{3}{4}$ of the mainmast; diameter $\frac{2}{3}$ of the main.

Main topmast is $\frac{3}{5}$ of the mainmast in length; its greatest diameter 1 inch to every 3 feet of length.

Fore topmast is $\frac{8}{9}$ of main topmast.

Mizzen topmast is $\frac{5}{7}$ of main topmast; its diameter is $\frac{7}{10}$ of main topmast.

Topgallant masts are $\frac{1}{2}$ the length of the topmasts, and their diameters are 1 inch to every 3 feet of length.

Royal masts are $\frac{3}{4}$ of the topmast in length, and their diameters are $\frac{2}{3}$ that of the topgallant masts.

The whole length of the bowsprit is $\frac{3}{7}$ that of the mainmast, $\frac{3}{4}$ of its length is outboard beyond the knightheads. Its diameter is the same as the foremast.

Jib boom, outboard, is the same length as the outboard part of the bowsprit, and its diameter is 1 inch to every 2½ feet of length.

Flying jib boom, outboard, equals 5/7 of the jib boom; its diameter is 7/8 inch to every 3 feet of length.

The main yard, total length, is 7/8 of the mainmast; its diameter .7 inch to 3 feet.

Fore yard is 7/8 of the main yard.

Crossjack yard is the same as the fore-topsail yard; its diameter 5/8 inch to 3 feet.

Main-topsail yard is 5/7 of main yard; its diameter 5/8 inch to 3 feet.

Fore-topsail yard is 7/8 of main-topsail yard.

Mizzen-topsail yard is 2/3 of the main-topsail yard.

Topgallant yard is 3/5 of topsail yard.

Royal yard is ½ of topsail yard.

Mizzen (spanker) boom, the same as main-topsail yard.

Mizzen gaff is 5/8 of the boom, its diameter is 5/8 inch to 3 feet.

This spanker boom, being figured for a ship, will be too short for a brig and will have to be increased to bring it just beyond the taffrail.

Now that we have the lengths of the spars, which I have drawn out in diagrammatic shape for convenience, and know their largest diameters as long practice has determined was a safe size, we want to know how to shape them, to give them the proper taper. This is furnished us in a very convenient and compact way by the following table:

SPAR PROPORTIONS

Spar	QUARTERS			HEAD		Heel
	First	Second	Third	Upper Part	Lower Part	
Lower masts	$\frac{60}{61}$	$\frac{14}{15}$	$\frac{6}{7}$	$\frac{3}{4}$	$\frac{5}{8}$	$\frac{6}{7}$
Top, t.gal. and royal masts	$\frac{60}{61}$	$\frac{14}{15}$	$\frac{6}{7}$	$\frac{9}{13}$	$\frac{6}{11}$	
Yards	$\frac{30}{31}$	$\frac{7}{8}$	$\frac{7}{10}$	$\frac{3}{7}$ *(Arms)*		
Bowsprits	$\frac{60}{61}$	$\frac{11}{12}$	$\frac{4}{5}$	$\frac{2}{3}$		$\frac{6}{7}$ *(Outer End)*
Jib boom and driver booms	$\frac{40}{41}$	$\frac{11}{12}$	$\frac{5}{6}$	$\frac{2}{3}$ *(Ends)*		
Main booms	$\frac{40}{41}$	$\frac{12}{13}$	$\frac{7}{8}$	$\frac{2}{3}$ *(Fore End)*	$\frac{3}{4}$ *(Aft End)*	$1\frac{1}{12}$ *(Middle)*
Gaffs	$\frac{40}{41}$	$\frac{11}{12}$	$\frac{4}{5}$	$\frac{5}{9}$		

Step-heeling, standing masts, $\frac{2}{3}$ athwartships, $\frac{1}{2}$ fore and aft. Step-heeling, bowsprit, $\frac{7}{19}$ athwartships, $\frac{2}{3}$ up and down.

To use this rule take our mainmast as an example. It is 56.4 feet long, but 10 feet of its lower end is under the deck where the greatest diameter is to be at the partners, and at the masthead 7.7 feet more where it is squared are both to be deducted from the total length of 56.4. So $10 \times 7.7 = 17.7$ and this from 56.4 leaves us 38.7 feet that is to be tapered. Divide this into four quarters ($38.7 \div 4 = 9.7$) and we have the spots where the table shows us what diameters they should be. At the deck we start with its known diameter of 18 inches. So measure up from the deck 9.7 feet to the first quarter where it is $\frac{60}{61}$ of 18 or $17\frac{3}{4}$ inches in diameter; another 9.7 feet to the second quarter and it is $\frac{14}{15}$ inches and so on.

I did not have to calculate all the proportions as there are tables with them all calculated and printed for ready reference by sparmakers in a little book by Robert Kipping entitled "Masting and Rigging," so for convenience I looked up the taper diameters for all the spars and give them herewith. (See page diagram.)

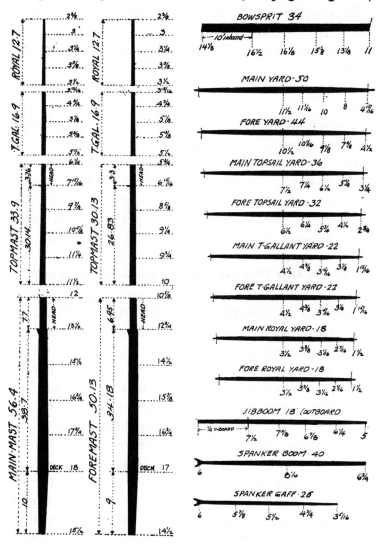

We cannot, however, proceed with the sparmaking yet for we do not know the length of the mastheads. They are as follows:

PROPORTION OF HEADS AND HOUNDS OF MASTS

Main and foremast heads, 5 inches per yard (3 feet) of length of mast.

Mizzenmast heads (if steps in hold), 4⅛ inches per yard.

All topmasts and topgallant mastheads, 4 inches per yard.

Length of hounds (below trestletrees), ⅖ of their respective heads.

Our mainmast 56.4 feet is 18.8 yards and at 5 inches per yard our brig's mainmast head would be 94 inches or 7 feet 10 inches long. There is a great deal of character in a well-made mast. Less, perhaps, in a single tree spar, such as our little brig would have, than in a built-up mast, composed of several trees shaped, coaked and banded together into one spar, where the chaplings show. But don't do what I have seen too many model-makers do, use a ready-turned out dowel that looks no more like a mast than a chair rung does. Make it of straight-grained split white pine, eight square at the deck, and let it stay so but tapered in size at the heel or step. Taper it eight square all the way to the hounds at first, so you are sure you get the proper taper and size and then plane down the corners into a round. Leave it octagonal for a couple of feet above the deck, and down from the hounds, a foot or so, then square the head from the hounds to the cap. It is the cheeks, trestle-trees, bolster and battens to take the crush of the shrouds on the sides of the masthead from the bolsters up as high as the collars of the rigging goes, and a cleat or two on the mast near the deck that makes a mast picturesque.

Getting the proper proportions to the tops, caps, and

trestletrees is just as important and you can get them so by using the following rules:

Proportions for Tops: Breadth, $\frac{1}{3}$ length of topmast. Length, fore and aft, $\frac{3}{4}$ of breadth. Lubbers hole (square), 5 inches to the foot.

Proportions for Caps: All caps, except jib boom, to be in breadth twice the diameter of topmasts and in length twice their breadth. Thickness of fore and main caps, $\frac{1}{2}$ of their breadth. Mizzen caps, $\frac{3}{7}$, and topmast caps, $\frac{2}{5}$ of their respective breadth.

Proportions for Trestletrees: In length to reach within 3 inches of outer edge of top. Depth of fore and main trestletrees, $\frac{25}{26}$ inch to foot in length. Breadth, $\frac{5}{7}$ of depth. Main and foretop mast trestletrees in length, $\frac{1}{5}$ length of topgallant mast; depth, $\frac{25}{26}$ inch per foot in length; breadth, $\frac{18}{25}$ of depth.

Proportions of Crosstrees: Length of fore and main crosstrees to reach within 3 inches of outer edge of top. Crosstrees same breadth as trestletrees and $\frac{1}{2}$ their depth.

Proportions of Topmast Trestletrees and Crosstrees: The length of trestletrees are $\frac{2}{5}$ the length of the lower crosstrees; breadth, $\frac{1}{2}$ the depth of the lower crosstrees; depth is $\frac{1}{2}$ the depth of lower crosstrees. Length of after crosstrees is $\frac{3}{5}$ that of the lower crosstrees. Length of the middle one $\frac{5}{6}$ of after one, length of forward one $\frac{5}{6}$ of middle one; breadth is the breadth of their respective trestletrees; depth or thickness $\frac{4}{5}$ of their breadth.

Our brig should have five lower shrouds; three topmast shrouds, two topgallant shrouds and to guide you in selecting the proper-sized ropes for your brig's standing rigging we can do no better than quote you from an old book the rule of 1755 in "Ship Builder's Assistant," by William Sutherland.

"Fore shrouds: circumference = $\frac{2}{7}$ diameter of mast at partners; pendants = the same; runners for tackles = $1\frac{1}{12}$ of pendant; tackle falls = $\frac{1}{2}$ pendants.

Forestay: circumference = $\frac{1}{2}$ diameter of foremast; lanyard = $\frac{7}{12}$ of the stay; lifts and braces = $\frac{1}{2}$ shrouds.

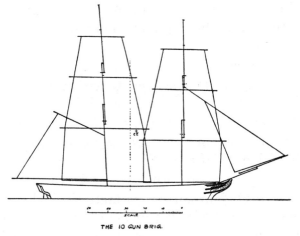

THE 10 GUN BRIG.

Fore topmast shrouds: circumference = $\frac{1}{3}$ diameter of topmasts; futtock shrouds = $\frac{7}{12}$ of shrouds; standing backstays = shrouds.

Fore topmast stay: circumference = $\frac{9}{25}$ of diameter of fore topmast; staysail stay = $\frac{7}{9}$ stay; lifts = $\frac{5}{9}$ stay; braces = same as lifts.

Fore topgallant shrouds: circumference = $\frac{2}{5}$ diameter of mast; stay = $\frac{3}{4}$ shrouds; lifts and braces = $\frac{1}{2}$ shrouds.

Mainmast shrouds: circumference = $\frac{9}{22}$ of diameter of mast at partners; lifts = $\frac{7}{16}$ of shrouds; braces = $\frac{6}{7}$ of the lifts; stay = $\frac{1}{2}$ diameter of mast.

Main topmast shrouds: circumference = $\frac{6}{29}$ diameter mast in the cap; ratlines = $\frac{2}{9}$ shrouds; stay = same as shrouds; staysail stay = $\frac{1}{9}$ stay.

Runners for topsail halliards: circumference = ½ diameter of topsail yard; halliards = ⅗ runners; lifts = 5⁄9 stays; runners and braces = same as lifts. Main topgallant shrouds: circumference = 5⁄9 topmast shrouds; futtocks = the same; stay = ¾ shrouds; tye = shrouds; halliards = ⅗ tye; braces = ⅔ lifts; lifts = halliards."

Plan and Dimensions of Spars on a 10-Gun British Brig-of-War

From John Edye's book entitled "On the Equipment and Displacement of Ships of War," published in 1832. Her hull dimensions are very similar to those of our little brig.

Length, 90 feet.

Length of keel, for tonnage, 73 feet, 7⅛ inches.

Beam, for tonnage, 24 feet, 6 inches.

Beam, extreme, 24 feet, 8 inches.

Depth of hold, 11 feet.

Tonnage, 235 tons.

Loaded draught, forward, 11 feet, 4 inches.

Loaded draught, aft, 14 feet, 7 inches.

Mainmast, length, 54 feet, 6 inches; 17¾ inches diameter.

Foremast, length, 46 feet, 6 inches; 16 inches diameter.

Bowsprit, length, 36 feet; 17 inches diameter.

Main topmast, length, 31 feet, 10 inches diameter.

Main topgallant mast, length, 19 feet, 6 inches; 6 inches diameter.

Main yard, length, 48 feet, 11 inches; 11 inches diameter.

Main topsail yard, length, 37 feet, 6 inches, 8 inches diameter.

Main topgallant yard, length, 26 feet, 6 inches diameter.

Foremasts, yards, etc., same as on mainmast.

Driver boom, length, 50 feet, 8 inches; 11 inches diameter.

Driver gaff, length, 30 feet, 4 inches; $7\frac{1}{2}$ inches diameter.

Jib boom, length, 27 feet; 8 inches diameter.

Spritsail yard, length, 37 feet, 6 inches; 8 inches diameter.

Foremast $\frac{5}{29}$ and mainmast $\frac{20}{31}$ of length on the L. W. L.

FORM OF A CONTRACT

Entered into by a Merchant-Ship Builder for the Building of a Ship of War for the Royal Navy including the Dimensions, &c., of the "RAVEN" Brig of 18 Guns, Built in the year 1804.

Contracted and agreed upon the _____ day of _____ in the year of our Lord 1804, by and between _____ Ship-builder of the one part, and _____ being three of the principal officers and Commissioners of His Majesty's Navy (for and on behalf of His Majesty, his heirs and successors) of the other part, that is to say as follows: First, the said _____ doth hereby for himself, his heirs, executors and administrators, covenant, contract and engage, at his own costs, charges, and expenses, to build in the yard at _____ in a substantial and workmanlike manner, and with good sound and proper materials of every kind. To be approved of by such officer or officers as shall from time to time be appointed to the principal offices and commissions of His Majesty's Navy for the time being, to superintend or inspect the same, a Brigantine for His Majesty to carry 16 Cannonades, 32 pounds, and two six-pounder guns, agreeably to the draught delivered to him for that purpose, in the manner and according to the condition, dimensions and scantlings following, viz.:

LENGTH. On the main deck from the after side of the stern to the fore side of the sternpost 100 feet 0 inches, of the keel for Tonnage 77 feet 3½ inches.

HEIGHT of the cutting down in midships 19½ inches.

BREADTH EXTREME. From out to outside of 3-inch plank, above the wale 30 feet 6 inches, moulded 30 feet 0 inchces, moulded at the height breadth at the aftermost part of the counter 17 feet 10½ inches, moulded at the top-timber or under side of the plank-sheer in midship 29 feet 6 inches; at the stern timber 16 feet 9 inches.

DEPTH IN HOLD. From the upper side of the strake next the limbers to the upper side of the main deck beam at the middle 12 feet 9 inches, strake next the limber boards thick 3 inches, broad 9 inches, distance from the keelson 8 inches.

BURTHEN in Tons — No. 382 $^{41}/_{94}$.

Rake of the stem and and stem post to be agreeable to the draught.

HEIGHT of the main deck from the upper side of the straight line at the upper side of the main keel to upper side of the plank of the deck at the stem, 14 feet 7 inches, ditto at the sternpost 18 feet 3 inches.

Of Breadth above the upper side of the main.

Keel in midships 13 feet 7 inches.

Of the Portsills from the upper side of the Upper Deck to the upper side of the Portsills 16 inches. Of the waist from the upper side of the keel to the under side of the plank, sheer-afore 20 feet, midships 19 feet, abaft 22 feet 7½ inches.

The Materials, Scantlings, Scarphing, &c. to be as follows, viz.:

KEEL. The Keel to be of elm, nor more than 4 pieces sided in midships, 11 inches at the fore end, 10 inches at the rabbets of the post 10 inches, to be 12 inches deep, the scarphs to be 3 feet 0 inches in length, bolted with 6 bolts of ⅞ of an inch in diameter.

FALSE KEEL. To have a false keel of elm 5½ inches in thickness, to have copper put between the main and false keels, and the sides and bottom thereof to be coppered as shall be directed, and sufficiently fastened with nails and staples.

STEM. The Stem to be in two pieces of good sound oak timber, sided at the head 16 inches, at the deck 11 inches, and at the forefoot the bigness of the keel, and moulded as described on the draught.

APRON. To be in thickness as described on the draught, and of breadth at least 16 inches.

STERNPOST. To run up and bolt to the upper deck transom, and as much higher as necessary, to be square at the head 13 inches. Fore and aft at the upper edge of the keel 2 feet 4 inches; abaft the rabbet at the wing transom 9 inches and the keel 1 foot 9 inches.

INNER POST to run up to the under side of the wing Transom, and to be 7½ inches fore and aft there, and 9½ inches on the keel; to be the same athwartships at the head as at the main post.

FASHION PIECES. To be sided 11 inches; rabbeted on the outside to receive the plank of the bottom on the aft side to receive the plank of the tuck.

WING TRANSOM. To be raised up 3½ inches and to cant forward 6½ inches, and square; to be sided 9½ inches and moulded 14 inches, to be rabbeted in the aft side to receive the plank of the tuck and plank of the counter, to have a knee at each end sided 6 inches, the arms of sufficient length and bolted as shall be directed.

RISING AND DEADWOOD, or thick stuff upon the keel in midships to be oak or elm of 8 inches thick and 13 inches broad, and of deadwood afore and abaft of a sufficient depth on the lower piece of which is to be a knee, and another apron, or under the keelson as shown on the draught; and the whole well fastened at every 20 inches distance by bolts of 1⅛ inches diameter.

BOLLARD TIMBERS. To have proper Bollard Timbers on each side, the stem for supporting the bowsprit; sided 9½ inches to cast or open sufficient to receive the diameter of the bowsprit.

ROOM AND SPACE of the Timbers 2 feet 4⅜ inches full, or as the stanchions of the frames on the draught.

FLOOR TIMBERS to be of oak or elm between D. and C. in midships, to be sided 9½ inches, and form thence fore and aft 9 inches, and to be in length in midships 12 feet 0 inches afore and abaft, as draught directs, and not to have less than 12 in whole wood below the cutting down and every floor timber to be bolted with bolts of copper through the keelson and main keel by bolts of 1⅛ inch diameter, and all the bolts to be carefully clenched on the underside of the main keel before the false keel is put under. To be moulded at the Heads 7½ inches.

LOWER FUTTOCKS. To be oak or fir. The nine midship timbers to be sided 8¾ inches, and thence forward and aft 8 inches, to scarph to the second futtock in midships 4 feet 10 inches, and afore and abaft as the draught directs to be moulded at the head 6¾. The lower futtocks for the better dividing of the frame are to be put between the floor so as to leave an equal opening on each side.

SECOND FUTTOCKS. To be oak or fir. Sided in midships 8 inches and afore and abaft 7¾ inches, moulded at the head 6½ inches; to scarph to the Futtocks in midships 4 feet 10 inches.

THIRD FUTTOCKS. To be oak or fir. All those appointed to make the side of a port are to be oak, sided in midships 8 inches and afore and abaft 7½ inches, moulded at the end 6¼, and to give scarph to top-timbers in midships 4 feet 10 inches and afore and aft as the draught directs.

TOP-TIMBERS to be oak or fir, the top-timbers in midships sided 8 inches and afore and abaft 7½ inches, and moulded at the head 5½ inches, and in the range of the deck at the side 6 inches.

FRAME. The whole of the port timbers are to be of oak, the other parts of the frame (except the floor) may be oak or fir, all fir to be Riga or Dantric of the very best quality.

HAWSE PIECES. To have three hawse pieces on each side, the foremost and aftermost to be sided 14½ inches, and the middle one 14½ inches, the hawse holes to be 10½ inches diameter in the clear, after the head scuppers are put in, and 11 inches asunder, the scupper not to be less than ⅝ inch thick at the lower part.

KEELSON. To be oak 11 inches square, to give good shift to the scarphs of the keel, and bolted through every floor timber by bolts 1⅛ inches in diameter, the scarphs to be 4 feet 8 inches long, wrought with hook and butt, all the bolts carefully clenched under the main keel, and to have a knee upon the after end thereof, bolts likewise to be copper.

WALES to be oak or fir, to have two strakes of main Wales 4½ inches thick and 12 inches in breadth, and to have 1 strake of 3½ inch thick stuff next upon, and 1 strake of 3½ inch thick stuff next under the main Wale to diminish 3 inches at the lower edge of the second strake; to be fastened with treenails.

PLANK OF THE BOTTOM. From the second strake next the wale downwards to be 3-inch fir plank wrought carved work of regular breadths, not less than 6 foot shifts of butts, to have a copper bolt in the winding edge of each strake, the bolts to be driven in the timber next the cut timber to be fastened with treenails.

The openings between the timbers are to be filled in and caulked inside and out from the floorheads downward.

To have copper bolts from the wales down, and above iron ¾ inch diameter, topside from the lower edge of the strake of the wale to diminish to 2 inches at the lower edge of the sheer strake which is to work down to the ports in midships. The sheer strakes to be 3-inch fir plank and that both wales and stuff upon and under that which covers the bottom be good sound well-seasoned fir plank, free from sap and all kinds of defects.

PLANK SHEER to be in thickness 3 inches thick, with a moulding on the outside to form a rail.

THICK STUFF IN HOLD. To have one strake of 3 inches and 9 inches broad, and 8 inches from the keelson on each side for a watercourse to the pump, with proper limber boards &c. as usual.

FLOORHEADS. To have 1 strake of 2½-inch plank and 9 inches broad wrought on the joints of the Timbers at the floor heads, and one of 2 inches thick and 9 inches broad, below and above them, which three strakes may be reduced to two strakes afore and abaft of 2 inches thick.

FIRST FUTTOCK HEADS to have one strake of 2½ inches

thick and 9 inches broad above and below it, which these strakes may be reduced to one afore and abaft $1\frac{1}{2}$ inches thick.

Lower Deck Clamps to have one strake of lower deck clamps on each side, 3 inches thick and 10 inches.

Pillars in hold under the lower deck beams to be 7 inches square at the lower and 6 inches at the upper end, those under the upper deck to be $6\frac{1}{2}$ inches at the lower end and 6 inches at the upper end, those under the upper deck to be handsomely turned.

Clamps to the main deck to be fir in two strakes, the upper $3\frac{1}{2}$ inches thick and 12 inches broad, the lower 3 inches thick and 10 inches broad, which two strakes may be reduced to one at the apron and fashion piece to 10 inches broad.

Ceiling all the rest of the Ceiling between the clamps and stuff at the floor heads and from thence down to be $1\frac{1}{2}$ inches thick, well wrought, and fastened, to be all fir.

Breast Hooks. The deck hook to be oak, sided $8\frac{1}{2}$ inches, and 11 feet 0 inches long, bolted with 7 bolts of $\frac{7}{8}$ inch diameter, and to have three breast hooks under the deck hook of oak, well disposed, so as best to strengthen the bow-sided 8 inches and not less than 8 feet in length, bolted the same as the deck breast hook. All the breast hook and knees of the head to be fastened with copper bolts.

Works in Hold and on the Platform and Lower Deck to fit proper steps for the main and foremast; lay a platform with beams, etc., as shew in the draught, beams sided $8\frac{1}{2}$ inches, moulded $6\frac{1}{2}$ inches, beams to be of fir, to be kneed with one lodge knee at each end of oak, sided $4\frac{1}{2}$ inches. To part off a well round the pumps with a locker at the fore or after part. To part off and finish with joiners work on the platform, the cabins and bed places for the commander and other officers, and also part off and make such necessary conveniences for head boatswain's carpenters and gunners' stores as shall be required and directed by the proper officers inspecting the same. Height from the plank of lower deck to upper deck beam at the middle line 5 feet 8 inches. Height of the after platform from the upper side of the plank or deal to upper side of upper deck beam 6 feet 2 inches.

MAIN DECK BEAMS to wind 9 inches in the greatest length to be in number and disposed as on the draught to be sided 10 inches and moulded 7¾ inches, the two after beams to be sided 9 inches and moulded 6¾ inches, and all to be of fir.

KNEES. The beams of the main deck to be kneed at each end with one hanging and one lodging knee of oak, the hanging knee to be sided 6 inches, bolted with eight bolts of ⅞ inch diameter, the up and down arm to be not less than 4 feet 0 inches and the athwartship one 3 feet, the lodging knee sided 5½ inches and the arms in proportion to the hanging, and as the room between the beams will require the whole of the knees to be so well grown that only the sap is to be taken from the throats, and great care is to be taken that they are not forced or graincut, and for the better securing the vessel by the knees the athwartship arm of the hanging knees is to be bolted with four fore and aft bolts, with iron plates let in on both sides of the beam to receive the second bolt from the crown of the knee, and the toe bolt, all the in and out bolts to be flat or tool headed.

CARLINGS AND LEDGES to have two tier of carlings on each side of the main deck, of fir 6 inches broad, 5½ inches deep, and ledges properly placed of 3¾ inches broad, 3¼ deep.

COAMINGS to all the hatches and scuttles on the upper deck to be at least 13 inches above the deck, and to be all fitted with close hatchets or gratings as shall be required.

WATER WAYS AND FLAT to be English oak plank of 4 inches thick, one strake next them, and one strake on each side next the coamings to be also of oak, all the rest of the flat of the deck to be laid with well-seasoned Prussia deals of 3 inches thick.

PORTS to have nine ports on each side for cannonade, as also a bow and stern chase as shew on the draught, the sills from the deck to be 16 inches to be fore and aft 2 feet 9 inches, and deep 2 feet 6 inches, to have two ring- and two eyebolts to each port of $1\frac{1}{8}$ inches diameter, the rings $3\frac{1}{2}$ inches diameter in the clear and those on the deck $\frac{3}{4}$ inch diameter; and also for stoppers $1\frac{1}{8}$ inches diameter, those through the side to be carefully clenched on a countersunk plate, and those through the deck to be carefully clenched under the beams.

SPICKETTING. The spicketting on each side to be of fir 3 inches thick, bolted with a $\frac{1}{4}$ inch bolt in the timber next the butt.

STRING. To have a string wrought fir three inches thick, to work down to the ports in midships, and to be continued of that breadth fore and aft, to shut in between the string and spicketting, with 2-inch fir plank, the ends at the port turned off with a quarter round, also the lower edge of the string and upper edge of the spicketting.

BREAST HOOK under the bowsprit to be oak sided $6\frac{1}{2}$ inches, the arms of sufficient length and bolted with seven or eight bolts of $\frac{7}{8}$ inch diameter.

BITTS to have a pair of riding bitts of oak, as shown on the draught and plans square at the deck $10\frac{1}{2}$ inches, the crosspiece of the dimensions and height from the deck as shown on the draught.

RIDERS to five riders on each side of oak, three against the main and two against the foremast, sided $9\frac{1}{2}$ inches.

CAPSTAN placed as shown on draught, the diameter in the partners 14 inches to be fitted with ribs and hoops at the partners, with eight or ten bars, chains, and two iron pauls on the deck.

SCUPPERS to have eight leaden scuppers on each, 4 inches diameter in the clear, carefully let out, and turned, that no leakage be found in the caps thereof.

MAIN AND FORE PARTNERS for the main and foremasts to be 6 inches thick, scored down 1 inch upon the beams of 3 feet 8 inches in breadth, and sufficiently bolted.

TIMBERHEADS, &c. To fit timberheads for stoppers, Catheads, bitts for jears, with chestrees and blocks, stopper bolts

on the flat of the deck, and other parts for rigging and everything that shall be required as necessary for an armed Brigantine.

CHANNELS for the main and foremasts described on the
draught of oak to be of sufficient breadth to carry the shrouds
12 inches clear of the hammock stanchion, the inner edge of
them to be 4 inches, the outer 3½ inches, and channel to be
bolted with six bolts of ¾ inch diameter, to have backstay
stools as shall be directed.

DEADEYES on each side, six for main channel 10 inches in
diameter, and five on each side of same diameter, for the fore
Channel, with such others to spare for backstays as shall be
required, and fitted with chains and preventer plates as shown
on the draught, the binding to be 1⅛ inches in diameter, those
of the backstays to be ⅞ inch diameter, the chain bolts to be
1¼ inches in diameter, and the presenter bolts 1⅛ inches in
diameter.

HORSE on TAFFRAIL TRANSOM. To have a horse for the
main sheet of wood made by the Taffrail Transom sided 6½
inches, and a block in the side for the fore sheet with a Transom Knee wrought at each end sided 4½ inches, the arm
next the lower side 5 feet 6 inches long, the other 4 feet 6
inches being bolted with ⅞ inch diameter.

ROTHER HEAD to be athwartships 14 inches fore, aft 14½
inches at the lower end, to be 3 feet 8 inches on a square —
the head to be well secured with hoops and plates, fitted with
a wood tiller of a proper length for steering the vessel.
Bearded as shown on the draught, the main piece to be of
oak and all the rest of fir.

STEERING WHEEL. To make and fit.

ROTHER IRONS. Five pair fitted in the securest manner
usual to vessels of her size, one pair to be above the deck, those
under water to be of copper or such metal as may be directed,
and to be found by His Majesty, and whatever weight they
may be, the value thereof is to be deducted from the contractor's bill, as in the case of the copper bolts.

COUNTER AND STERN timbers whole and properly placed, to make the stern ports with security for the ensign staff transom for the main sheet, properly kneed, and other services required, and to have a neat plain taffrail and quarter pieces as usual.

HEAD. To have a scroll head with cheeks and rail, as shown on the draught, to be properly fashioned, and as shall be derected, knees of the Head to be oak.

IRON WORK to be wrought out of the best iron, not burnt or hurt in working, and that all the bolts shall be either clinched or forelocked, and the rings let into the wood.

N. B. The iron for the channels, ring- and eyebolts for the posts, top tackle bolts, stopper bolts, or any additional iron work which the Commissioner of the Navy may direct, is to be supplied by them, the said Commissioners, and the amount to be deducted from the contractor's final bill at the rate last paid to the contractor for iron, previous to its being delivered to them.

COPPER BOLTS are to be found by His Majesty, and whatever the weight of them may be, the value of the same weight in iron is to be abated of the contractor's bill, at the rate of 1£ 10 per cwt. after deducting $\frac{1}{8}$ weight of copper, this difference being found to be in the weight of copper more than iron of similar dimension.

CAULKING. The vessels sides and bottom to be carefully caulked in every seam and butt of $4\frac{1}{2}$ inches, six double threads of black oakum and two of spun yarn, and in every seam and butt of 4 inches five double threads of black oakum, and two of spun yarn, and in every seam and butt of 3 inches four double threads of black oakum and one of spun yarn. All black oakum to be picked out of good junk and the whole to be good sound oakum, the spun yarn to be of leather, save for the above purpose.

PAINTING. To treble paint or pay the bottom with tar boiled a strong consistence, to treble paint the vessel with good oil colors from the wales up, and within the spicketting and capstan companion, steering-wheel, coamings, hame knees, cabins and clamps, with what else is usual for such vessels.

TIME OF LAUNCHING, and the said further covenants, promises, contracts, and agrees, to and with the said principal officers of the Navy (parties hereto) that the said Brigantine shall be completed, launched, and delivered safe afloat into the hands of such officer or officers as by the Commissioners of His Majesty's Navy for the time being shall be appointed to receive her by or before the expiration of three Calendar Months, to be computed from the 29th of May 1804.

IF ORDERED TO STAND TO SEASON. It is agreed by and between the said parties that if the Commissioners of His Majesty's Navy for the time being shall think it expedient when the frame of the said Brig is completed, that it should stand still in order to season the said _____ in that case (upon notice thereof from said Commissioner) to cease all further progress for and during the time mentioned in such notice, but to be allowed in addition to the three calendar months above mentioned, as much further time for completing and delivering the said Brig as aforesaid, as he shall be destrained by the said notice from prosecuting the work.

DEFECTS TO BE AMENDED. Provided also that if any material or workmanship shall by the officer or officers so to be appointed to by the officer or officers so to be appointed to inspect the same as aforesaid be deemed defective, unsound, improper, or insufficient, then and in such case the _____ from time to time and as often as the same shall happen, is to cause all such defects and insufficiencies to be forthwith amended or altered, as the case may require to, to the satisfaction and good liking of said officer or officers.

RATA PER TON. In consideration whereof the said commissioners (parties hereto) do hereby for and on behalf of His Majesty, promise and agree that the said _____ sum shall be paid for the said Brigantine, after the rate of 19£ 10S. per Ton, namely, for so many Tons as the Brigantine shall measure, not exceeding 382⁴¹⁄₉₄ Tons, but not for any greater number of Tons, unless any increase of scantlings and dimensions shall be made in pursuance of an order in writing under the hands of three or more of the principal commissioners of His Majesty's Navy, for the time being and such rate of Tonnage is hereby declared and agreed to be, the full and entire compensation and payment for the said Brigantine, without any other charge or expense whatsoever.

PAYMENTS. The said rate each Ton to be paid in manner and form following, viz.:

First, a Bill of Import to be made out to _____ for the sum 1460£, on signing this contract.

Second, Another for the sum of 1460£, when the keel is laid, the floor timbers across the stern, and stern frame bends raised, the lower futtock cocked across and keelson bolted.

Third, Another for the sum of 1460£ more when all the timbers of the frame are in the bottom, planked, the wales about the footwailing and clamps wrought, and lower deck beams in their places.

Fourth, Another for the sum of 1460£ more when all the beams of the upper deck are in, the decks laid, the Brig planked up within and without board, the works in hold finished and the knee of the head up.

A PERFECT BILL for the remainder that shall be due for the said Brigantine, deducting therefrom the value of the weight in iron of the copper bolts, also the value of the iron as hereinbefore directed, and after she shall be entirely completed and launched safely afloat as aforesaid into the hands of such officer or officers appointed to receive her (and the draught and contract by which she was built returned to the Navy office) and a certificate of the performance of the whole work according to the tenure of this contract, made and given by such person or persons as shall be appointed by the said principal officers and commissioners, all which bills are to be paid in ninety days from their date, with interest thereon at the rate of 3 pence per cent per diem.

BILLS TO BE STOPPED. Provided always, nevertheless, and

it is hereby agreed by and between the said parties that although imprest bills are hereinbefore mentioned to be made out as the works of the said Brigantine shall progress or go on, it may be lawful to and for the said Commissioners for His Majesty's Navy, to stop such of the said bills as shall not happen to be assigned for payment, when as often as it shall appear to the inspecting officer or officers that any of the works, the said Brigantine have not been executed or carried on agreeably to the time, intent and meaning of this contract.

IN CASE OF FAILURE. And, lastly, it is hereby also agreed by and between the said parties that if the said _____ shall fail or neglect to carry on and complete the said Brigantine conformably to his engagement hereinbefore mentioned, then and in such case as much of the said Brigantine as shall be done at the time of such failure or neglect shall be the property of His Majesty, upon the said principal officers of His Majesty's Navy, for the time being, paying for the same according to the usual value of such works what shall be found to be due to the said _____ after deducting the amount of such Imprest Bill or Bills as shall have been made out and delivered to him, pending the progress of the said works. And in case of failure or neglect, it shall be lawful to and for the said Commissioners with workmen and others to enter into the yard or dock where the said Brigantine shall be building, and either to take away the said Brigantine, or employ workmen to finish the same and for that purpose to bring in all proper materials and do all things necessary for completing the said Brigantine and also to launch the same for His Majesty's use, without any molestation or hinderance whatsoever from the said _____ his executors, administrators or assigns, without making any allowance or compensation by way of rent or otherwise, for the use of the said yard or dock. In Witness Whereof the said parties to these presents have hereunto interchangeably set their hands and seals, the day and year first before written or mentioned:

Sealed and delivered (being
   first duly stamped)
   in the presence of _____

Provided, nevertheless, that in case the said Brigantine shall
be completed and launched within the three months mentioned in the aforegoing contract, then the said Commissioners
do agree that the said_____shall be allowed a premium of
5s. per ton for every week she shall be completed and
launched within the aforegoing three months, but it is to be
understood that no addition shall be made to the 19£ 10s. per
Ton mentioned in the aforegoing contract, if she shall be
launched and completed in less than one week within the
aforesaid time.

INDEX

A CATALOG OF SELECTED

DOVER BOOKS

IN ALL FIELDS OF INTEREST

A CATALOG OF SELECTED DOVER
BOOKS IN ALL FIELDS OF INTEREST

DRAWINGS OF REMBRANDT, edited by Seymour Slive. Updated Lippmann, Hofstede de Groot edition, with definitive scholarly apparatus. All portraits, biblical sketches, landscapes, nudes. Oriental figures, classical studies, together with selection of work by followers. 550 illustrations. Total of 630pp. 9⅛ × 12¼.
21485-0, 21486-9 Pa., Two-vol. set $29.90

GHOST AND HORROR STORIES OF AMBROSE BIERCE, Ambrose Bierce. 24 tales vividly imagined, strangely prophetic, and decades ahead of their time in technical skill: "The Damned Thing," "An Inhabitant of Carcosa," "The Eyes of the Panther," "Moxon's Master," and 20 more. 199pp. 5⅜ × 8½. 20767-6 Pa. $4.95

ETHICAL WRITINGS OF MAIMONIDES, Maimonides. Most significant ethical works of great medieval sage, newly translated for utmost precision, readability. Laws Concerning Character Traits, Eight Chapters, more. 192pp. 5⅜ × 8½.
24522-5 Pa. $4.50

THE EXPLORATION OF THE COLORADO RIVER AND ITS CANYONS, J. W. Powell. Full text of Powell's 1,000-mile expedition down the fabled Colorado in 1869. Superb account of terrain, geology, vegetation, Indians, famine, mutiny, treacherous rapids, mighty canyons, during exploration of last unknown part of continental U.S. 400pp. 5⅜ × 8½. 20094-9 Pa. $7.95

HISTORY OF PHILOSOPHY, Julián Marías. Clearest one-volume history on the market. Every major philosopher and dozens of others, to Existentialism and later. 505pp. 5⅜ × 8½. 21739-6 Pa. $9.95

ALL ABOUT LIGHTNING, Martin A. Uman. Highly readable non-technical survey of nature and causes of lightning, thunderstorms, ball lightning, St. Elmo's Fire, much more. Illustrated. 192pp. 5⅜ × 8½. 25237-X Pa. $5.95

SAILING ALONE AROUND THE WORLD, Captain Joshua Slocum. First man to sail around the world, alone, in small boat. One of great feats of seamanship told in delightful manner. 67 illustrations. 294pp. 5⅜ × 8½. 20326-3 Pa. $4.95

LETTERS AND NOTES ON THE MANNERS, CUSTOMS AND CONDITIONS OF THE NORTH AMERICAN INDIANS, George Catlin. Classic account of life among Plains Indians: ceremonies, hunt, warfare, etc. 312 plates. 572pp. of text. 6⅛ × 9¼. 22118-0, 22119-9, Pa. Two-vol. set $17.90

ALASKA: The Harriman Expedition, 1899, John Burroughs, John Muir, et al. Informative, engrossing accounts of two-month, 9,000-mile expedition. Native peoples, wildlife, forests, geography, salmon industry, glaciers, more. Profusely illustrated. 240 black-and-white line drawings. 124 black-and-white photographs. 3 maps. Index. 576pp. 5⅜ × 8½. 25109-8 $11.95

THE BOOK OF BEASTS: Being a Translation from a Latin Bestiary of the Twelfth Century, T. H. White. Wonderful catalog real and fanciful beasts: manticore, griffin, phoenix, amphivius, jaculus, many more. White's witty erudite commentary on scientific, historical aspects. Fascinating glimpse of medieval mind. Illustrated. 296pp. 5⅜ × 8¼. (Available in U.S. only)   24609-4 Pa. $6.95

FRANK LLOYD WRIGHT: ARCHITECTURE AND NATURE With 160 Illustrations, Donald Hoffmann. Profusely illustrated study of influence of nature—especially prairie—on Wright's designs for Fallingwater, Robie House, Guggenheim Museum, other masterpieces. 96pp. 9¼ × 10¾.   25098-9 Pa. $8.95

FRANK LLOYD WRIGHT'S FALLINGWATER, Donald Hoffmann. Wright's famous waterfall house: planning and construction of organic idea. History of site, owners, Wright's personal involvement. Photographs of various stages of building. Preface by Edgar Kaufmann, Jr. 100 illustrations. 112pp. 9¼ × 10.

23671-4 Pa. $8.95

YEARS WITH FRANK LLOYD WRIGHT: Apprentice to Genius, Edgar Tafel. Insightful memoir by a former apprentice presents a revealing portrait of Wright the man, the inspired teacher, the greatest American architect. 372 black-and-white illustrations. Preface. Index. vi + 228pp. 8¼ × 11.   24801-1 Pa. $10.95

THE STORY OF KING ARTHUR AND HIS KNIGHTS, Howard Pyle. Enchanting version of King Arthur fable has delighted generations with imaginative narratives of exciting adventures and unforgettable illustrations by the author. 41 illustrations. xviii + 313pp. 6⅛ × 9¼.   21445-1 Pa. $6.95

THE GODS OF THE EGYPTIANS, E. A. Wallis Budge. Thorough coverage of numerous gods of ancient Egypt by foremost Egyptologist. Information on evolution of cults, rites and gods; the cult of Osiris; the Book of the Dead and its rites; the sacred animals and birds; Heaven and Hell; and more. 956pp. 6⅛ × 9¼.
22055-9, 22056-7 Pa., Two-vol. set $21.90

A THEOLOGICO-POLITICAL TREATISE, Benedict Spinoza. Also contains unfinished *Political Treatise*. Great classic on religious liberty, theory of government on common consent. R. Elwes translation. Total of 421pp. 5⅜ × 8½.
20249-6 Pa. $7.95

INCIDENTS OF TRAVEL IN CENTRAL AMERICA, CHIAPAS, AND YUCATAN, John L. Stephens. Almost single-handed discovery of Maya culture; exploration of ruined cities, monuments, temples; customs of Indians. 115 drawings. 892pp. 5⅜ × 8½.   22404-X, 22405-8 Pa., Two-vol. set $15.90

LOS CAPRICHOS, Francisco Goya. 80 plates of wild, grotesque monsters and caricatures. Prado manuscript included. 183pp. 6⅜ × 9⅜.   22384-1 Pa. $5.95

AUTOBIOGRAPHY: The Story of My Experiments with Truth, Mohandas K. Gandhi. Not hagiography, but Gandhi in his own words. Boyhood, legal studies, purification, the growth of the Satyagraha (nonviolent protest) movement. Critical, inspiring work of the man who freed India. 480pp. 5⅜ × 8½. (Available in U.S. only)
24593-4 Pa. $6.95

ILLUSTRATED DICTIONARY OF HISTORIC ARCHITECTURE, edited by Cyril M. Harris. Extraordinary compendium of clear, concise definitions for over 5,000 important architectural terms complemented by over 2,000 line drawings. Covers full spectrum of architecture from ancient ruins to 20th-century Modernism. Preface. 592pp. 7½ × 9⅝. 24444-X Pa. $15.95

THE NIGHT BEFORE CHRISTMAS, Clement Moore. Full text, and woodcuts from original 1848 book. Also critical, historical material. 19 illustrations. 40pp. 4⅝ × 6. 22797-9 Pa. $2.50

THE LESSON OF JAPANESE ARCHITECTURE: 165 Photographs, Jiro Harada. Memorable gallery of 165 photographs taken in the 1930's of exquisite Japanese homes of the well-to-do and historic buildings. 13 line diagrams. 192pp. 8⅜ × 11¼. 24778-3 Pa. $10.95

THE AUTOBIOGRAPHY OF CHARLES DARWIN AND SELECTED LETTERS, edited by Francis Darwin. The fascinating life of eccentric genius composed of an intimate memoir by Darwin (intended for his children); commentary by his son, Francis; hundreds of fragments from notebooks, journals, papers; and letters to and from Lyell, Hooker, Huxley, Wallace and Henslow. xi + 365pp. 5⅜ × 8. 20479-0 Pa. $6.95

WONDERS OF THE SKY: Observing Rainbows, Comets, Eclipses, the Stars and Other Phenomena, Fred Schaaf. Charming, easy-to-read poetic guide to all manner of celestial events visible to the naked eye. Mock suns, glories, Belt of Venus, more. Illustrated. 299pp. 5¼ × 8¼. 24402-4 Pa. $7.95

BURNHAM'S CELESTIAL HANDBOOK, Robert Burnham, Jr. Thorough guide to the stars beyond our solar system. Exhaustive treatment. Alphabetical by constellation: Andromeda to Cetus in Vol. 1; Chamaeleon to Orion in Vol. 2; and Pavo to Vulpecula in Vol. 3. Hundreds of illustrations. Index in Vol. 3. 2,000pp. 6⅛ × 9¼. 23567-X, 23568-8, 23673-0 Pa., Three-vol. set $41.85

STAR NAMES: Their Lore and Meaning, Richard Hinckley Allen. Fascinating history of names various cultures have given to constellations and literary and folkloristic uses that have been made of stars. Indexes to subjects. Arabic and Greek names. Biblical references. Bibliography. 563pp. 5⅜ × 8½. 21079-0 Pa. $8.95

THIRTY YEARS THAT SHOOK PHYSICS: The Story of Quantum Theory, George Gamow. Lucid, accessible introduction to influential theory of energy and matter. Careful explanations of Dirac's anti-particles, Bohr's model of the atom, much more. 12 plates. Numerous drawings. 240pp. 5⅜ × 8½. 24895-X Pa. $5.95

CHINESE DOMESTIC FURNITURE IN PHOTOGRAPHS AND MEASURED DRAWINGS, Gustav Ecke. A rare volume, now affordably priced for antique collectors, furniture buffs and art historians. Detailed review of styles ranging from early Shang to late Ming. Unabridged republication. 161 black-and-white drawings, photos. Total of 224pp. 8⅜ × 11¼. (Available in U.S. only) 25171-3 Pa. $13.95

VINCENT VAN GOGH: A Biography, Julius Meier-Graefe. Dynamic, penetrating study of artist's life, relationship with brother, Theo, painting techniques, travels, more. Readable, engrossing. 160pp. 5⅜ × 8½. (Available in U.S. only) 25253-1 Pa. $4.95

HOW TO WRITE, Gertrude Stein. Gertrude Stein claimed anyone could understand her unconventional writing—here are clues to help. Fascinating improvisations, language experiments, explanations illuminate Stein's craft and the art of writing. Total of 414pp. 4⅜ × 6⅜. 23144-5 Pa. $6.95

ADVENTURES AT SEA IN THE GREAT AGE OF SAIL: Five Firsthand Narratives, edited by Elliot Snow. Rare true accounts of exploration, whaling, shipwreck, fierce natives, trade, shipboard life, more. 33 illustrations. Introduction. 353pp. 5⅜ × 8½. 25177-2 Pa. $8.95

THE HERBAL OR GENERAL HISTORY OF PLANTS, John Gerard. Classic descriptions of about 2,850 plants—with over 2,700 illustrations—includes Latin and English names, physical descriptions, varieties, time and place of growth, more. 2,706 illustrations. xlv + 1,678pp. 8½ × 12¼. 23147-X Cloth. $75.00

DOROTHY AND THE WIZARD IN OZ, L. Frank Baum. Dorothy and the Wizard visit the center of the Earth, where people are vegetables, glass houses grow and Oz characters reappear. Classic sequel to *Wizard of Oz.* 256pp. 5⅜ × 8. 24714-7 Pa. $5.95

SONGS OF EXPERIENCE: Facsimile Reproduction with 26 Plates in Full Color, William Blake. This facsimile of Blake's original "Illuminated Book" reproduces 26 full-color plates from a rare 1826 edition. Includes "The Tyger," "London," "Holy Thursday," and other immortal poems. 26 color plates. Printed text of poems. 48pp. 5¼ × 7. 24636-1 Pa. $3.95

SONGS OF INNOCENCE, William Blake. The first and most popular of Blake's famous "Illuminated Books," in a facsimile edition reproducing all 31 brightly colored plates. Additional printed text of each poem. 64pp. 5¼ × 7. 22764-2 Pa. $3.95

PRECIOUS STONES, Max Bauer. Classic, thorough study of diamonds, rubies, emeralds, garnets, etc.: physical character, occurrence, properties, use, similar topics. 20 plates, 8 in color. 94 figures. 659pp. 6⅛ × 9¼. 21910-0, 21911-9 Pa., Two-vol. set $15.90

ENCYCLOPEDIA OF VICTORIAN NEEDLEWORK, S. F. A. Caulfeild and Blanche Saward. Full, precise descriptions of stitches, techniques for dozens of needlecrafts—most exhaustive reference of its kind. Over 800 figures. Total of 679pp. 8⅛ × 11. Two volumes. Vol. 1 22800-2 Pa. $11.95
Vol. 2 22801-0 Pa. $11.95

THE MARVELOUS LAND OF OZ, L. Frank Baum. Second Oz book, the Scarecrow and Tin Woodman are back with hero named Tip, Oz magic. 136 illustrations. 287pp. 5⅜ × 8½. 20692-0 Pa. $5.95

WILD FOWL DECOYS, Joel Barber. Basic book on the subject, by foremost authority and collector. Reveals history of decoy making and rigging, place in American culture, different kinds of decoys, how to make them, and how to use them. 140 plates. 156pp. 7⅞ × 10¾. 20011-6 Pa. $8.95

HISTORY OF LACE, Mrs. Bury Palliser. Definitive, profusely illustrated chronicle of lace from earliest times to late 19th century. Laces of Italy, Greece, England, France, Belgium, etc. Landmark of needlework scholarship. 266 illustrations. 672pp. 6⅛ × 9¼. 24742-2 Pa. $14.95

ILLUSTRATED GUIDE TO SHAKER FURNITURE, Robert Meader. All furniture and appurtenances, with much on unknown local styles. 235 photos. 146pp. 9 × 12. 22819-3 Pa. $8.95

WHALE SHIPS AND WHALING: A Pictorial Survey, George Francis Dow. Over 200 vintage engravings, drawings, photographs of barks, brigs, cutters, other vessels. Also harpoons, lances, whaling guns, many other artifacts. Comprehensive text by foremost authority. 207 black-and-white illustrations. 288pp. 6 × 9. 24808-9 Pa. $9.95

THE BERTRAMS, Anthony Trollope. Powerful portrayal of blind self-will and thwarted ambition includes one of Trollope's most heartrending love stories. 497pp. 5⅜ × 8½. 25119-5 Pa. $9.95

ADVENTURES WITH A HAND LENS, Richard Headstrom. Clearly written guide to observing and studying flowers and grasses, fish scales, moth and insect wings, egg cases, buds, feathers, seeds, leaf scars, moss, molds, ferns, common crystals, etc.—all with an ordinary, inexpensive magnifying glass. 209 exact line drawings aid in your discoveries. 220pp. 5⅜ × 8½. 23330-8 Pa. $4.95

RODIN ON ART AND ARTISTS, Auguste Rodin. Great sculptor's candid, wide-ranging comments on meaning of art; great artists; relation of sculpture to poetry, painting, music; philosophy of life, more. 76 superb black-and-white illustrations of Rodin's sculpture, drawings and prints. 119pp. 8⅜ × 11¼. 24487-3 Pa. $7.95

FIFTY CLASSIC FRENCH FILMS, 1912–1982: A Pictorial Record, Anthony Slide. Memorable stills from Grand Illusion, Beauty and the Beast, Hiroshima, Mon Amour, many more. Credits, plot synopses, reviews, etc. 160pp. 8¼ × 11. 25256-6 Pa. $11.95

THE PRINCIPLES OF PSYCHOLOGY, William James. Famous long course complete, unabridged. Stream of thought, time perception, memory, experimental methods; great work decades ahead of its time. 94 figures. 1,391pp. 5⅜ × 8½. 20381-6, 20382-4 Pa., Two-vol. set $23.90

BODIES IN A BOOKSHOP, R. T. Campbell. Challenging mystery of blackmail and murder with ingenious plot and superbly drawn characters. In the best tradition of British suspense fiction. 192pp. 5⅜ × 8½. 24720-1 Pa. $4.95

CALLAS: PORTRAIT OF A PRIMA DONNA, George Jellinek. Renowned commentator on the musical scene chronicles incredible career and life of the most controversial, fascinating, influential operatic personality of our time. 64 black-and-white photographs. 416pp. 5⅜ × 8¼. 25047-4 Pa. $8.95

GEOMETRY, RELATIVITY AND THE FOURTH DIMENSION, Rudolph Rucker. Exposition of fourth dimension, concepts of relativity as Flatland characters continue adventures. Popular, easily followed yet accurate, profound. 141 illustrations. 133pp. 5⅜ × 8½. 23400-2 Pa. $4.95

HOUSEHOLD STORIES BY THE BROTHERS GRIMM, with pictures by Walter Crane. 53 classic stories—Rumpelstiltskin, Rapunzel, Hansel and Gretel, the Fisherman and his Wife, Snow White, Tom Thumb, Sleeping Beauty, Cinderella, and so much more—lavishly illustrated with original 19th century drawings. 114 illustrations. x + 269pp. 5⅜ × 8½. 21080-4 Pa. $4.95

CATALOG OF DOVER BOOKS

SUNDIALS, Albert Waugh. Far and away the best, most thorough coverage of ideas, mathematics concerned, types, construction, adjusting anywhere. Over 100 illustrations. 230pp. 5⅜ × 8½. 22947-5 Pa. $5.95

PICTURE HISTORY OF THE NORMANDIE: With 190 Illustrations, Frank O. Braynard. Full story of legendary French ocean liner: Art Deco interiors, design innovations, furnishings, celebrities, maiden voyage, tragic fire, much more. Extensive text. 144pp. 8⅞ × 11¾. 25257-4 Pa. $10.95

THE FIRST AMERICAN COOKBOOK: A Facsimile of "American Cookery," 1796, Amelia Simmons. Facsimile of the first American-written cookbook published in the United States contains authentic recipes for colonial favorites— pumpkin pudding, winter squash pudding, spruce beer, Indian slapjacks, and more. Introductory Essay and Glossary of colonial cooking terms. 80pp. 5⅜ × 8½. 24710-4 Pa. $3.50

101 PUZZLES IN THOUGHT AND LOGIC, C. R. Wylie, Jr. Solve murders and robberies, find out which fishermen are liars, how a blind man could possibly identify a color—purely by your own reasoning! 107pp. 5⅜ × 8½. 20367-0 Pa. $2.50

ANCIENT EGYPTIAN MYTHS AND LEGENDS, Lewis Spence. Examines animism, totemism, fetishism, creation myths, deities, alchemy, art and magic, other topics. Over 50 illustrations. 432pp. 5⅜ × 8½. 26525-0 Pa. $8.95

ANTHROPOLOGY AND MODERN LIFE, Franz Boas. Great anthropologist's classic treatise on race and culture. Introduction by Ruth Bunzel. Only inexpensive paperback edition. 255pp. 5⅜ × 8½. 25245-0 Pa. $6.95

THE TALE OF PETER RABBIT, Beatrix Potter. The inimitable Peter's terrifying adventure in Mr. McGregor's garden, with all 27 wonderful, full-color Potter illustrations. 55pp. 4¼ × 5½. (Available in U.S. only) 22827-4 Pa. $1.75

THREE PROPHETIC SCIENCE FICTION NOVELS, H. G. Wells. *When the Sleeper Wakes, A Story of the Days to Come* and *The Time Machine* (full version). 335pp. 5⅜ × 8½. (Available in U.S. only) 20605-X Pa. $6.95

APICIUS COOKERY AND DINING IN IMPERIAL ROME, edited and translated by Joseph Dommers Vehling. Oldest known cookbook in existence offers readers a clear picture of what foods Romans ate, how they prepared them, etc. 49 illustrations. 301pp. 6⅛ × 9¼. 23563-7 Pa. $7.95

SHAKESPEARE LEXICON AND QUOTATION DICTIONARY, Alexander Schmidt. Full definitions, locations, shades of meaning of every word in plays and poems. More than 50,000 exact quotations. 1,485pp. 6½ × 9¼. 22726-X, 22727-8 Pa., Two-vol. set $31.90

THE WORLD'S GREAT SPEECHES, edited by Lewis Copeland and Lawrence W. Lamm. Vast collection of 278 speeches from Greeks to 1970. Powerful and effective models; unique look at history. 842pp. 5⅜ × 8½. 20468-5 Pa. $12.95

THE BLUE FAIRY BOOK, Andrew Lang. The first, most famous collection, with many familiar tales: Little Red Riding Hood, Aladdin and the Wonderful Lamp, Puss in Boots, Sleeping Beauty, Hansel and Gretel, Rumpelstiltskin; 37 in all. 138 illustrations. 390pp. 5⅜ × 8½.   21437-0 Pa. $6.95

THE STORY OF THE CHAMPIONS OF THE ROUND TABLE, Howard Pyle. Sir Launcelot, Sir Tristram and Sir Percival in spirited adventures of love and triumph retold in Pyle's inimitable style. 50 drawings, 31 full-page. xviii + 329pp. 6½ × 9¼.   21883-X Pa. $7.95

THE MYTHS OF THE NORTH AMERICAN INDIANS, Lewis Spence. Myths and legends of the Algonquins, Iroquois, Pawnees and Sioux with comprehensive historical and ethnological commentary. 36 illustrations. 5⅜ × 8½.

25967-6 Pa. $8.95

GREAT DINOSAUR HUNTERS AND THEIR DISCOVERIES, Edwin H. Colbert. Fascinating, lavishly illustrated chronicle of dinosaur research, 1820's to 1960. Achievements of Cope, Marsh, Brown, Buckland, Mantell, Huxley, many others. 384pp. 5¼ × 8¼.   24701-5 Pa. $7.95

THE TASTEMAKERS, Russell Lynes. Informal, illustrated social history of American taste 1850's-1950's. First popularized categories Highbrow, Lowbrow, Middlebrow. 129 illustrations. New (1979) afterword. 384pp. 6 × 9.

23993-4 Pa. $8.95

DOUBLE CROSS PURPOSES, Ronald A. Knox. A treasure hunt in the Scottish Highlands, an old map, unidentified corpse, surprise discoveries keep reader guessing in this cleverly intricate tale of financial skullduggery. 2 black-and-white maps. 320pp. 5⅜ × 8½. (Available in U.S. only)   25032-6 Pa. $6.95

AUTHENTIC VICTORIAN DECORATION AND ORNAMENTATION IN FULL COLOR: 46 Plates from "Studies in Design," Christopher Dresser. Superb full-color lithographs reproduced from rare original portfolio of a major Victorian designer. 48pp. 9¼ × 12¼.   25083-0 Pa. $7.95

PRIMITIVE ART, Franz Boas. Remains the best text ever prepared on subject, thoroughly discussing Indian, African, Asian, Australian, and, especially, North-ern American primitive art. Over 950 illustrations show ceramics, masks, totem poles, weapons, textiles, paintings, much more. 376pp. 5⅜ × 8.   20025-6 Pa. $7.95

SIDELIGHTS ON RELATIVITY, Albert Einstein. Unabridged republication of two lectures delivered by the great physicist in 1920–21. *Ether and Relativity* and *Geometry and Experience.* Elegant ideas in non-mathematical form, accessible to intelligent layman. vi + 56pp. 5⅜ × 8½.   24511-X Pa. $2.95

THE WIT AND HUMOR OF OSCAR WILDE, edited by Alvin Redman. More than 1,000 ripostes, paradoxes, wisecracks: Work is the curse of the drinking classes, I can resist everything except temptation, etc. 258pp. 5⅜ × 8½.   20602-5 Pa. $4.95

ADVENTURES WITH A MICROSCOPE, Richard Headstrom. 59 adventures with clothing fibers, protozoa, ferns and lichens, roots and leaves, much more. 142 illustrations. 232pp. 5⅜ × 8½.   23471-1 Pa. $3.95

PLANTS OF THE BIBLE, Harold N. Moldenke and Alma L. Moldenke. Standard reference to all 230 plants mentioned in Scriptures. Latin name, biblical reference, uses, modern identity, much more. Unsurpassed encyclopedic resource for scholars, botanists, nature lovers, students of Bible. Bibliography. Indexes. 123 black-and-white illustrations. 384pp. 6 × 9. 25069-5 Pa. $8.95

FAMOUS AMERICAN WOMEN: A Biographical Dictionary from Colonial Times to the Present, Robert McHenry, ed. From Pocahontas to Rosa Parks, 1,035 distinguished American women documented in separate biographical entries. Accurate, up-to-date data, numerous categories, spans 400 years. Indices. 493pp. 6½ × 9¼. 24523-3 Pa. $10.95

THE FABULOUS INTERIORS OF THE GREAT OCEAN LINERS IN HISTORIC PHOTOGRAPHS, William H. Miller, Jr. Some 200 superb photographs capture exquisite interiors of world's great "floating palaces"—1890's to 1980's: *Titanic, Ile de France, Queen Elizabeth, United States, Europa,* more. Approx. 200 black-and-white photographs. Captions. Text. Introduction. 160pp. 8⅜ × 11¾. 24756-2 Pa. $9.95

THE GREAT LUXURY LINERS, 1927–1954: A Photographic Record, William H. Miller, Jr. Nostalgic tribute to heyday of ocean liners. 186 photos of Ile de France, Normandie, Leviathan, Queen Elizabeth, United States, many others. Interior and exterior views. Introduction. Captions. 160pp. 9 × 12. 24056-8 Pa. $10.95

A NATURAL HISTORY OF THE DUCKS, John Charles Phillips. Great landmark of ornithology offers complete detailed coverage of nearly 200 species and subspecies of ducks: gadwall, sheldrake, merganser, pintail, many more. 74 full-color plates, 102 black-and-white. Bibliography. Total of 1,920pp. 8⅜ × 11¼. 25141-1, 25142-X Cloth. Two-vol. set $100.00

THE SEAWEED HANDBOOK: An Illustrated Guide to Seaweeds from North Carolina to Canada, Thomas F. Lee. Concise reference covers 78 species. Scientific and common names, habitat, distribution, more. Finding keys for easy identification. 224pp. 5⅜ × 8½. 25215-9 Pa. $6.95

THE TEN BOOKS OF ARCHITECTURE: The 1755 Leoni Edition, Leon Battista Alberti. Rare classic helped introduce the glories of ancient architecture to the Renaissance. 68 black-and-white plates. 336pp. 8⅜ × 11¼. 25239-6 Pa. $14.95

MISS MACKENZIE, Anthony Trollope. Minor masterpieces by Victorian master unmasks many truths about life in 19th-century England. First inexpensive edition in years. 392pp. 5⅜ × 8½. 25201-9 Pa. $8.95

THE RIME OF THE ANCIENT MARINER, Gustave Doré, Samuel Taylor Coleridge. Dramatic engravings considered by many to be his greatest work. The terrifying space of the open sea, the storms and whirlpools of an unknown ocean, the ice of Antarctica, more—all rendered in a powerful, chilling manner. Full text. 38 plates. 77pp. 9¼ × 12. 22305-1 Pa. $4.95

THE EXPEDITIONS OF ZEBULON MONTGOMERY PIKE, Zebulon Montgomery Pike. Fascinating first-hand accounts (1805–6) of exploration of Mississippi River, Indian wars, capture by Spanish dragoons, much more. 1,088pp. 5⅜ × 8½. 25254-X, 25255-8 Pa. Two-vol. set $25.90

CATALOG OF DOVER BOOKS

A CONCISE HISTORY OF PHOTOGRAPHY: Third Revised Edition, Helmut Gernsheim. Best one-volume history—camera obscura, photochemistry, daguerreotypes, evolution of cameras, film, more. Also artistic aspects—landscape, portraits, fine art, etc. 281 black-and-white photographs. 26 in color. 176pp. 8⅜ × 11¼. 25128-4 Pa. $13.95

THE DORÉ BIBLE ILLUSTRATIONS, Gustave Doré. 241 detailed plates from the Bible: the Creation scenes, Adam and Eve, Flood, Babylon, battle sequences, life of Jesus, etc. Each plate is accompanied by the verses from the King James version of the Bible. 241pp. 9 × 12. 23004-X Pa. $9.95

WANDERINGS IN WEST AFRICA, Richard F. Burton. Great Victorian scholar/adventurer's invaluable descriptions of African tribal rituals, fetishism, culture, art, much more. Fascinating 19th-century account. 624pp. 5⅜ × 8½. 26890-X Pa. $12.95

FLATLAND, E. A. Abbott. Intriguing and enormously popular science-fiction classic explores the complexities of trying to survive as a two-dimensional being in a three-dimensional world. Amusingly illustrated by the author. 16 illustrations. 103pp. 5⅜ × 8½. 20001-9 Pa. $2.50

THE HISTORY OF THE LEWIS AND CLARK EXPEDITION, Meriwether Lewis and William Clark, edited by Elliott Coues. Classic edition of Lewis and Clark's day-by-day journals that later became the basis for U.S. claims to Oregon and the West. Accurate and invaluable geographical, botanical, biological, meteorological and anthropological material. Total of 1,508pp. 5⅜ × 8½. 21268-8, 21269-6, 21270-X Pa. Three-vol. set $26.85

LANGUAGE, TRUTH AND LOGIC, Alfred J. Ayer. Famous, clear introduction to Vienna, Cambridge schools of Logical Positivism. Role of philosophy, elimination of metaphysics, nature of analysis, etc. 160pp. 5⅜ × 8½. (Available in U.S. and Canada only) 20010-8 Pa. $3.95

MATHEMATICS FOR THE NONMATHEMATICIAN, Morris Kline. Detailed, college-level treatment of mathematics in cultural and historical context, with numerous exercises. For liberal arts students. Preface. Recommended Reading Lists. Tables. Index. Numerous black-and-white figures. xvi + 641pp. 5⅜ × 8½. 24823-2 Pa. $11.95

HANDBOOK OF PICTORIAL SYMBOLS, Rudolph Modley. 3,250 signs and symbols, many systems in full; official or heavy commercial use. Arranged by subject. Most in Pictorial Archive series. 143pp. 8⅛ × 11. 23357-X Pa. $6.95

INCIDENTS OF TRAVEL IN YUCATAN, John L. Stephens. Classic (1843) exploration of jungles of Yucatan, looking for evidences of Maya civilization. Travel adventures, Mexican and Indian culture, etc. Total of 669pp. 5⅜ × 8½. 20926-1, 20927-X Pa., Two-vol. set $11.90

DEGAS: An Intimate Portrait, Ambroise Vollard. Charming, anecdotal memoir by famous art dealer of one of the greatest 19th-century French painters. 14 black-and-white illustrations. Introduction by Harold L. Van Doren. 96pp. 5⅜ × 8½.
25131-4 Pa. $4.95

PERSONAL NARRATIVE OF A PILGRIMAGE TO ALMANDINAH AND MECCAH, Richard Burton. Great travel classic by remarkably colorful personality. Burton, disguised as a Moroccan, visited sacred shrines of Islam, narrowly escaping death. 47 illustrations. 959pp. 5⅜ × 8½.   21217-3, 21218-1 Pa., Two-vol. set $19.90

PHRASE AND WORD ORIGINS, A. H. Holt. Entertaining, reliable, modern study of more than 1,200 colorful words, phrases, origins and histories. Much unexpected information. 254pp. 5⅜ × 8½.   20758-7 Pa. $5.95

THE RED THUMB MARK, R. Austin Freeman. In this first Dr. Thorndyke case, the great scientific detective draws fascinating conclusions from the nature of a single fingerprint. Exciting story, authentic science. 320pp. 5⅜ × 8½. (Available in U.S. only)   25210-8 Pa. $6.95

AN EGYPTIAN HIEROGLYPHIC DICTIONARY, E. A. Wallis Budge. Monumental work containing about 25,000 words or terms that occur in texts ranging from 3000 B.C. to 600 A.D. Each entry consists of a transliteration of the word, the word in hieroglyphs, and the meaning in English. 1,314pp. 6⅜ × 10.
23615-3, 23616-1 Pa., Two-vol. set $35.90

THE COMPLEAT STRATEGYST: Being a Primer on the Theory of Games of Strategy, J. D. Williams. Highly entertaining classic describes, with many illustrated examples, how to select best strategies in conflict situations. Prefaces. Appendices. xvi + 268pp. 5⅜ × 8½.   25101-2 Pa. $6.95

THE ROAD TO OZ, L. Frank Baum. Dorothy meets the Shaggy Man, little Button-Bright and the Rainbow's beautiful daughter in this delightful trip to the magical Land of Oz. 272pp. 5⅜ × 8.   25208-6 Pa. $5.95

POINT AND LINE TO PLANE, Wassily Kandinsky. Seminal exposition of role of point, line, other elements in non-objective painting. Essential to understanding 20th-century art. 127 illustrations. 192pp. 6½ × 9¼.   23808-3 Pa. $5.95

LADY ANNA, Anthony Trollope. Moving chronicle of Countess Lovel's bitter struggle to win for herself and daughter Anna their rightful rank and fortune—perhaps at cost of sanity itself. 384pp. 5⅜ × 8½.   24669-8 Pa. $8.95

EGYPTIAN MAGIC, E. A. Wallis Budge. Sums up all that is known about magic in Ancient Egypt: the role of magic in controlling the gods, powerful amulets that warded off evil spirits, scarabs of immortality, use of wax images, formulas and spells, the secret name, much more. 253pp. 5⅜ × 8½.   22681-6 Pa. $4.50

THE DANCE OF SIVA, Ananda Coomaraswamy. Preeminent authority unfolds the vast metaphysic of India: the revelation of her art, conception of the universe, social organization, etc. 27 reproductions of art masterpieces. 192pp. 5⅜ × 8½.
24817-8 Pa. $5.95

CHRISTMAS CUSTOMS AND TRADITIONS, Clement A. Miles. Origin, evolution, significance of religious, secular practices. Caroling, gifts, yule logs, much more. Full, scholarly yet fascinating; non-sectarian. 400pp. 5⅜ × 8½.
23354-5 Pa. $6.95

THE HUMAN FIGURE IN MOTION, Eadweard Muybridge. More than 4,500 stopped-action photos, in action series, showing undraped men, women, children jumping, lying down, throwing, sitting, wrestling, carrying, etc. 390pp. 7⅞ × 10⅝.
20204-6 Cloth. $24.95

THE MAN WHO WAS THURSDAY, Gilbert Keith Chesterton. Witty, fast-paced novel about a club of anarchists in turn-of-the-century London. Brilliant social, religious, philosophical speculations. 128pp. 5⅜ × 8½. 25121-7 Pa. $3.95

A CEZANNE SKETCHBOOK: Figures, Portraits, Landscapes and Still Lifes, Paul Cezanne. Great artist experiments with tonal effects, light, mass, other qualities in over 100 drawings. A revealing view of developing master painter, precursor of Cubism. 102 black-and-white illustrations. 144pp. 8¾ × 6⅜. 24790-2 Pa. $6.95

AN ENCYCLOPEDIA OF BATTLES: Accounts of Over 1,560 Battles from 1479 B.C. to the Present, David Eggenberger. Presents essential details of every major battle in recorded history, from the first battle of Megiddo in 1479 B.C. to Grenada in 1984. List of Battle Maps. New Appendix covering the years 1967–1984. Index. 99 illustrations. 544pp. 6½ × 9¼. 24913-1 Pa. $14.95

AN ETYMOLOGICAL DICTIONARY OF MODERN ENGLISH, Ernest Weekley. Richest, fullest work, by foremost British lexicographer. Detailed word histories. Inexhaustible. Total of 856pp. 6½ × 9¼.
21873-2, 21874-0 Pa., Two-vol. set $19.90

WEBSTER'S AMERICAN MILITARY BIOGRAPHIES, edited by Robert McHenry. Over 1,000 figures who shaped 3 centuries of American military history. Detailed biographies of Nathan Hale, Douglas MacArthur, Mary Hallaren, others. Chronologies of engagements, more. Introduction. Addenda. 1,033 entries in alphabetical order. xi + 548pp. 6½ × 9¼. (Available in U.S. only)
24758-9 Pa. $13.95

LIFE IN ANCIENT EGYPT, Adolf Erman. Detailed older account, with much not in more recent books: domestic life, religion, magic, medicine, commerce, and whatever else needed for complete picture. Many illustrations. 597pp. 5⅜ × 8½.
22632-8 Pa. $8.95

HISTORIC COSTUME IN PICTURES, Braun & Schneider. Over 1,450 costumed figures shown, covering a wide variety of peoples: kings, emperors, nobles, priests, servants, soldiers, scholars, townsfolk, peasants, merchants, courtiers, cavaliers, and more. 256pp. 8⅜ × 11¼. 23150-X Pa. $9.95

THE NOTEBOOKS OF LEONARDO DA VINCI, edited by J. P. Richter. Extracts from manuscripts reveal great genius; on painting, sculpture, anatomy, sciences, geography, etc. Both Italian and English. 186 ms. pages reproduced, plus 500 additional drawings, including studies for *Last Supper, Sforza* monument, etc. 860pp. 7⅞ × 10¾. (Available in U.S. only) 22572-0, 22573-9 Pa., Two-vol. set $31.90

CATALOG OF DOVER BOOKS

THE ART NOUVEAU STYLE BOOK OF ALPHONSE MUCHA: All 72 Plates from "Documents Decoratifs" in Original Color, Alphonse Mucha. Rare copyright-free design portfolio by high priest of Art Nouveau. Jewelry, wallpaper, stained glass, furniture, figure studies, plant and animal motifs, etc. Only complete one-volume edition. 80pp. 9⅜ × 12¼.   24044-4 Pa. $9.95

ANIMALS: 1,419 COPYRIGHT-FREE ILLUSTRATIONS OF MAMMALS, BIRDS, FISH, INSECTS, ETC., edited by Jim Harter. Clear wood engravings present, in extremely lifelike poses, over 1,000 species of animals. One of the most extensive pictorial sourcebooks of its kind. Captions. Index. 284pp. 9 × 12.
                                                                              23766-4 Pa. $9.95

OBELISTS FLY HIGH, C. Daly King. Masterpiece of American detective fiction, long out of print, involves murder on a 1935 transcontinental flight—"a very thrilling story"—NY Times. Unabridged and unaltered republication of the edition published by William Collins Sons & Co. Ltd., London, 1935. 288pp. 5⅜ × 8½. (Available in U.S. only)   25036-9 Pa. $5.95

VICTORIAN AND EDWARDIAN FASHION: A Photographic Survey, Alison Gernsheim. First fashion history completely illustrated by contemporary photographs. Full text plus 235 photos, 1840–1914, in which many celebrities appear. 240pp. 6½ × 9¼.   24205-6 Pa. $8.95

THE ART OF THE FRENCH ILLUSTRATED BOOK, 1700–1914, Gordon N. Ray. Over 630 superb book illustrations by Fragonard, Delacroix, Daumier, Doré, Grandville, Manet, Mucha, Steinlen, Toulouse-Lautrec and many others. Preface. Introduction. 633 halftones. Indices of artists, authors & titles, binders and provenances. Appendices. Bibliography. 608pp. 8⅜ × 11¼.   25086-5 Pa. $24.95

THE WONDERFUL WIZARD OF OZ, L. Frank Baum. Facsimile in full color of America's finest children's classic. 143 illustrations by W. W. Denslow. 267pp. 5⅜ × 8½.   20691-2 Pa. $7.95

FOLLOWING THE EQUATOR: A Journey Around the World, Mark Twain. Great writer's 1897 account of circumnavigating the globe by steamship. Ironic humor, keen observations, vivid and fascinating descriptions of exotic places. 197 illustrations. 720pp. 5⅜ × 8½.   26113-1 Pa. $15.95

THE FRIENDLY STARS, Martha Evans Martin & Donald Howard Menzel. Classic text marshalls the stars together in an engaging, non-technical survey, presenting them as sources of beauty in night sky. 23 illustrations. Foreword. 2 star charts. Index. 147pp. 5⅜ × 8½.   21099-5 Pa. $3.95

FADS AND FALLACIES IN THE NAME OF SCIENCE, Martin Gardner. Fair, witty appraisal of cranks, quacks, and quackeries of science and pseudoscience: hollow earth, Velikovsky, orgone energy, Dianetics, flying saucers, Bridey Murphy, food and medical fads, etc. Revised, expanded In the Name of Science. "A very able and even-tempered presentation."—The New Yorker. 363pp. 5⅜ × 8.
                                                                              20394-8 Pa. $6.95

ANCIENT EGYPT: ITS CULTURE AND HISTORY, J. E Manchip White. From pre-dynastics through Ptolemies: society, history, political structure, religion, daily life, literature, cultural heritage. 48 plates. 217pp. 5⅜ × 8½.   22548-8 Pa. $5.95

CATALOG OF DOVER BOOKS

SIR HARRY HOTSPUR OF HUMBLETHWAITE, Anthony Trollope. Incisive, unconventional psychological study of a conflict between a wealthy baronet, his idealistic daughter, and their scapegrace cousin. The 1870 novel in its first inexpensive edition in years. 250pp. 5⅜ × 8½. 24953-0 Pa. $6.95

LASERS AND HOLOGRAPHY, Winston E. Kock. Sound introduction to burgeoning field, expanded (1981) for second edition. Wave patterns, coherence, lasers, diffraction, zone plates, properties of holograms, recent advances. 84 illustrations. 160pp. 5⅜ × 8¼. (Except in United Kingdom) 24041-X Pa. $3.95

INTRODUCTION TO ARTIFICIAL INTELLIGENCE: SECOND, EN-LARGED EDITION, Philip C. Jackson, Jr. Comprehensive survey of artificial intelligence—the study of how machines (computers) can be made to act intelligently. Includes introductory and advanced material. Extensive notes updating the main text. 132 black-and-white illustrations. 512pp. 5⅜ × 8½. 24864-X Pa. $8.95

HISTORY OF INDIAN AND INDONESIAN ART, Ananda K. Coomaraswamy. Over 400 illustrations illuminate classic study of Indian art from earliest Harappa finds to early 20th century. Provides philosophical, religious and social insights. 304pp. 6⅜ × 9⅜. 25005-9 Pa. $11.95

THE GOLEM, Gustav Meyrink. Most famous supernatural novel in modern European literature, set in Ghetto of Old Prague around 1890. Compelling story of mystical experiences, strange transformations, profound terror. 13 black-and-white illustrations. 224pp. 5⅜ × 8½. (Available in U.S. only) 25025-3 Pa. $6.95

PICTORIAL ENCYCLOPEDIA OF HISTORIC ARCHITECTURAL PLANS, DETAILS AND ELEMENTS: With 1,880 Line Drawings of Arches, Domes, Doorways, Facades, Gables, Windows, etc., John Theodore Haneman. Sourcebook of inspiration for architects, designers, others. Bibliography. Captions. 141pp. 9 × 12. 24605-1 Pa. $7.95

BENCHLEY LOST AND FOUND, Robert Benchley. Finest humor from early 30's, about pet peeves, child psychologists, post office and others. Mostly unavailable elsewhere. 73 illustrations by Peter Arno and others. 183pp. 5⅜ × 8½. 22410-4 Pa. $4.95

ERTÉ GRAPHICS, Erté. Collection of striking color graphics: *Seasons, Alphabet, Numerals, Aces* and *Precious Stones*. 50 plates, including 4 on covers. 48pp. 9⅜ × 12¼. 23580-7 Pa. $7.95

THE JOURNAL OF HENRY D. THOREAU, edited by Bradford Torrey, F. H. Allen. Complete reprinting of 14 volumes, 1837–61, over two million words; the sourcebooks for *Walden*, etc. Definitive. All original sketches, plus 75 photographs. 1,804pp. 8½ × 12¼. 20312-3, 20313-1 Cloth., Two-vol. set $125.00

CASTLES: THEIR CONSTRUCTION AND HISTORY, Sidney Toy. Traces castle development from ancient roots. Nearly 200 photographs and drawings illustrate moats, keeps, baileys, many other features. Caernarvon, Dover Castles, Hadrian's Wall, Tower of London, dozens more. 256pp. 5⅜ × 8¼. 24898-4 Pa. $6.95

CATALOG OF DOVER BOOKS

AMERICAN CLIPPER SHIPS: 1833–1858, Octavius T. Howe & Frederick C. Matthews. Fully-illustrated, encyclopedic review of 352 clipper ships from the period of America's greatest maritime supremacy. Introduction. 109 halftones. 5 black-and-white line illustrations. Index. Total of 928pp. 5⅜ × 8½.

25115-2, 25116-0 Pa., Two-vol. set $17.90

TOWARDS A NEW ARCHITECTURE, Le Corbusier. Pioneering manifesto by great architect, near legendary founder of "International School." Technical and aesthetic theories, views on industry, economics, relation of form to function, "mass-production spirit," much more. Profusely illustrated. Unabridged translation of 13th French edition. Introduction by Frederick Etchells. 320pp. 6⅛ × 9¼. (Available in U.S. only) 25023-7 Pa. $8.95

THE BOOK OF KELLS, edited by Blanche Cirker. Inexpensive collection of 32 full-color, full-page plates from the greatest illuminated manuscript of the Middle Ages, painstakingly reproduced from rare facsimile edition. Publisher's Note. Captions. 32pp. 9⅜ × 12¼. 24345-1 Pa. $4.95

BEST SCIENCE FICTION STORIES OF H. G. WELLS, H. G. Wells. Full novel *The Invisible Man*, plus 17 short stories: "The Crystal Egg," "Aepyornis Island," "The Strange Orchid," etc. 303pp. 5⅜ × 8½. (Available in U.S. only)

21531-8 Pa. $6.95

AMERICAN SAILING SHIPS: Their Plans and History, Charles G. Davis. Photos, construction details of schooners, frigates, clippers, other sailcraft of 18th to early 20th centuries—plus entertaining discourse on design, rigging, nautical lore, much more. 137 black-and-white illustrations. 240pp. 6⅛ × 9¼.

24658-2 Pa. $6.95

ENTERTAINING MATHEMATICAL PUZZLES, Martin Gardner. Selection of author's favorite conundrums involving arithmetic, money, speed, etc., with lively commentary. Complete solutions. 112pp. 5⅜ × 8½. 25211-6 Pa. $2.95

THE WILL TO BELIEVE, HUMAN IMMORTALITY, William James. Two books bound together. Effect of irrational on logical, and arguments for human immortality. 402pp. 5⅜ × 8½. 20291-7 Pa. $7.95

THE HAUNTED MONASTERY and THE CHINESE MAZE MURDERS, Robert Van Gulik. 2 full novels by Van Gulik continue adventures of Judge Dee and his companions. An evil Taoist monastery, seemingly supernatural events; overgrown topiary maze that hides strange crimes. Set in 7th-century China. 27 illustrations. 328pp. 5⅜ × 8½. 23502-5 Pa. $6.95

CELEBRATED CASES OF JUDGE DEE (DEE GOONG AN), translated by Robert Van Gulik. Authentic 18th-century Chinese detective novel; Dee and associates solve three interlocked cases. Led to Van Gulik's own stories with same characters. Extensive introduction. 9 illustrations. 237pp. 5⅜ × 8½.

23337-5 Pa. $5.95

Prices subject to change without notice.
Available at your book dealer or write for free catalog to Dept. GI, Dover Publications, Inc., 31 East 2nd St., Mineola, N.Y. 11501. Dover publishes more than 175 books each year on science, elementary and advanced mathematics, biology, music, art, literary history, social sciences and other areas.